Praise for PERFORMANCE SCORECARDS

"*Performance Scorecards* offers managers at every level a roadmap and real world examples for turning data collection into organizational performance management on both the strategic and operations dimensions."

> —Trina Mullen, Vice President, Customer Information and Training Services, Nortel Networks

"*Performance Scorecards* contains highly relevant examples and is exceptionally engaging. The summary of steps and outcomes at the end of each chapter provides a useful checklist to ensure that all important issues are addressed in each phase. I would recommend this book to anyone who is struggling with how to measure performance or wants to do it better."

> —Dr. Katherine Holt, Vice President, Personnel Decisions International (PDI)

"Once again, Richard Chang Associates has produced a business management tool that is practical, useful, and applicable at every level of the organization. Most business managers say there's never enough time . . . make time for this."

> —Colleen Catallo, Vice President, Fidelity Investments

"Richard Chang Associates has done it again! They have taken 'what sounds good in theory' and translated it into a practical approach that I look forward to using in my work. *Performance Scorecards,* with its concise examples of how world-class leaders have benefited from these approaches, provides the tools to help companies that may have derailed in earlier quality improvement efforts, now refocus on what matters—and helps make the essential linkages between the boardroom and the front line."

> —Jan Ahrens John, Director, Organizational Development, The Regence Group

"Every leader who wants to establish clear goals, manage performance, and celebrate results will find immediate help in *Performance Scorecards*. Richard Chang and Mark Morgan have created one of the most useful guides yet for helping busy leaders focus on what really matters."

> —Craig R. Taylor, Director, Group Marketing and Sales, Disney Institute

"Anyone in business today will benefit from this book. It is easy to read and chock-full of practical tips and suggestions for how to identify, and collect information on, performance measures."

> —Dana Gaines Robinson, Co-Author of *Performance Consulting*

"*Performance Scorecards* reduces the anxiety and mystery of developing and implementing measurements by providing practical guidelines and realistic examples of how the process works and the pitfalls that will need to be addressed. This book will be an invaluable aid for future measurement training."

> —Bruce Rosenstiel, Manager, Quality Services, GTE Directories

"In today's business world of explosive change, effective results measurement is critical to success and continuous improvement. Start ups, as well as Fortune 500 companies, will benefit from the straightforward approach and the "how to" steps outlined in *Performance Scorecards*."
  —Bob Earnest, Vice President, E-Commerce, Herman Miller for the Home

"For all the executive leaders of a business, *Performance Scorecards* is a must read! At last there is a realistic template for determining, integrating, and aligning the measures of success for a business. This is a fun read with a powerful message!"
  —Laura Longmire, Vice President, Clarke American

"Any business, regardless of size or type, can benefit by following the six-phase approach outlined in this practical and easy-to-read book. *Performance Scorecards* provides a great way to measure and assess the pulse of an organization!"
  —Richard L. Blackstone, Director of Management and Team Training,
    The Reynolds and Reynolds Company

"As the speed of business continues to increase, access to timely information on the strategic measures that matter is becoming a critical component to long-term success. *Performance Scorecards* provides the step-by-step model to translate business strategy into day-to-day business decisions and actions."
  —Donnee Ramelli, Vice President, Learning and Organization Development,
    AlliedSignal, Inc.

"Organization leaders need a measurement model and the competencies to apply it while supporting the business and its performance needs. In *Performance Scorecards,* Richard Chang and Mark Morgan present a practical, business-focused model that breaks new ground in our efforts to demonstrate performance results."
  —Tom LaBonte, Human Resources Executive, Centura Banks, Inc.

"*Performance Scorecards* integrates the abstract concepts of measurement, strategic planning, and performance management into a cohesive, yet simple approach to achieving breakthrough business results. Years of experience wrestling with the REAL issues and working in the trenches have led to Richard Chang and Mark Morgan's uncanny ability to distill the daunting concept of measuring performance into a sensible approach to maximizing business performance."
  —Kimberly Janson, Director of Organizational Effectiveness and
    Workforce Diversity, Hasbro, Inc.

"*Performance Scorecards* addresses a subject critical to all of us in today's information overload world. That is, what and how to measure and how to then link this information to what is really important. The vignette style makes it easy to read and apply."
  —Gary Floss, Vice President, Corporate Quality, Medtronic, Inc.

PERFORMANCE SCORECARDS

PERFORMANCE SCORECARDS

Measuring the Right Things in the Real World

Richard Y. Chang – Mark W. Morgan

JOSSEY-BASS
A Wiley Company
San Francisco

Founded in 1977, the Houston-based American Productivity & Quality Center (APQC) provides organizations with the knowledge, training, and methods to help them improve productivity and quality. A nonprofit organization and a recognized leader in benchmarking, knowledge management and best-practice information, APQC serves its 500-plus international members in all sectors of business, industry, education, and government.

Manufactured in the United States of America.

Interior design by Paula Goldstein

Library of Congress Cataloging-in-Publication Data
Chang, Richard Y.
  Performance scorecards : measuring the right things in the real world / Richard Y. Chang, Mark W. Morgan.—1st ed.
      p.   cm.
Includes bibliographical references.
  ISBN 0-7879-5272-9 (alk. paper)
  1. Organizational effectiveness—Measurement. 2. Performance technology. I. Morgan, Mark W. II. Title.
  HD58.9 .C483 2000
  658.5'0028'7—dc21   99-050888

first edition

HB Printing   10 9 8 7 6 5 4 3 2 1

To my parents, William and Catherine, my sister and brother-in-law, Sophia and C.T., and niece, Kasen, for their unending love, support, and encouragement.

To the organizations, executives, managers, and employees around the world who continue to advocate that the measurement of performance is a key priority and continue to strive to figure out the right things to measure.

RICHARD CHANG

To my wife, Nancy, and my children, Catherine, Annie, and Max, for their immeasurable love and support.

To my parents, David and Anita, for always being there when it counted.

MARK MORGAN

Contents

The Authoring Team

Richard Chang is CEO of Richard Chang Associates, Inc., a diversified, performance improvement consulting, training, and publishing firm headquartered in Irvine, California. He is internationally recognized for his strategic planning, performance measurement, quality improvement, organization development, product realization, change management, customer service, and human resource development expertise. As an internal business practitioner, Chang previously held internal management and senior leadership positions in four organizations. He has served as an external consultant to a wide variety of organizations, including: Toshiba, Marriott, Citibank, McDonald's, Universal Studios, Fidelity Investments, Nabisco, and many others.

Chang has served as chair of the board for the American Society for Training and Development (ASTD), as a judge for the Malcolm Baldrige National Quality Award, and holds a Ph.D. in industrial/organizational psychology. He is the author or co-author of more than twenty books on business and personal development, including *The Passion Plan: A Step-by-Step Guide to Discovering, Developing, and Living Your Passion* (Jossey-Bass, 1999). Chang is a top-rated keynote speaker at conferences around the world and has been cited in *Outstanding Young Men of America, Who's Who in Leading American Executives,* and *International Who's Who in Quality.*

Mark Morgan is a senior consultant for Richard Chang Associates, Inc. Morgan has worked at all organizational levels on scorecard development, strategic planning, performance measurement, organizational assessment, team building, project management, and process improvement. He has consulted to Nortel Networks, BellSouth, Fidelity Investments, Northrop Grumman, Nabisco, Hasbro, DuPont, Boeing, Ford, Bank of New Zealand, NASA, Lockheed Martin, and many others.

As an internal quality and measurement specialist, Morgan has held a variety of leadership and management positions in business. He has a doctorate in educational leadership from the University of Florida and served on the Board of Examiners during 1999 and 1998 for the Malcolm Baldrige National Quality Award. He is a member of the American Society for Quality and has served on numerous national committees for the American Society for Training and Development. He is a published author and an award-winning public speaker.

Preface

There are three types of business leaders:

⇨   Those who know the score and know they are winning;

⇨   Those who know the score and know they are losing; and

⇨   Those who don't know the score.

Relying on a combined total of more than forty years of organizational measurement and improvement experience, the authoring team contends that most modern managers fall in the last category. Modern business managers thirst for knowledge while drowning in a sea of data.

Today's managers have access to more information than they need and struggle daily under a deluge of reports, e-mails, and briefings. While managing the information flood, managers have less time for analyzing, interpreting, and acting on results. Downsizing, competitive pressures, and momentary market opportunities add to the need to have immediate and actionable knowledge for making timely decisions.

Performance Scorecards address a wide variety of needs that managers, their team members, and their superiors have in order to manage and achieve performance results. Some of those needs and the solutions that the scorecards provide include:

⇨   *A demand for timely, easy-to-understand information.* Performance Scorecards provide a concise summary of critical measures needed for updates and decisions.

⇨   *A desire to see a graphic depiction of the performance of key measures.* Performance Scorecards allow the manager to monitor performance against targets, business goals, and competitive benchmarks.

⇨ *A need for timely information on the measures that matter.* The scorecards contain indicators that directly relate to decision making and business results.

Performance Scorecards can be presented electronically, on paper, or with large displays. The format is not critical. The most important aspect of Performance Scorecards is their linkage and alignment to business strategy and the use of the scorecards to evaluate the organization's health in critical areas quickly.

When fully developed, Performance Scorecards help business leaders slice through the clutter of today's information glut, providing decision tools that reduce time and expense for gathering and analyzing data. Performance Scorecards provide a picture of true performance that is concise, accurate, and current.

By reducing data overload, properly developed and deployed Performance Scorecards become a manager's tool for aligning business strategy and for promoting behaviors leading to desired results. The right measures in the right places reinforce business outcomes for customers, employees, managers, and other stakeholders.

Performance Scorecards enable companies to:

⇨ Drive achievement toward business goals;

⇨ Provide focus on business strategies;

⇨ Align employees' efforts toward objectives;

⇨ Sustain improved business performance;

⇨ Guide shifts in business direction; and

⇨ Achieve balanced results across stakeholder groups.

After years of working with many managers in many organizations, the team of consultants from Richard Chang Associates, Inc., has developed the methodology described in this book for developing meaningful and action-oriented Performance Scorecards. Using the techniques described herein, organizational leaders at all levels can create greater understanding of true business performance, easily identify problem areas, consistently communicate goals, track progress toward targets, and align efforts to achieve market-competitive performance levels.

A great deal of well-deserved business press has been devoted to Balanced Scorecards, introduced by Robert Kaplan and David Norton in articles in the *Harvard Business Review* and in their book, *The Balanced Scorecard.* Kaplan and Norton state that organizations can more effectively manage results with a balance of measures in four categories: "financial," "customer," "internal processes," and "learning and growth." When developed, a Balanced Scorecard becomes an instrument for aligning organizational performance with strategy.

The Performance Scorecards described within this book have the same advantages as Balanced Scorecards, with an important added distinction. While Balanced Scorecards typically have four categories of results, Performance Scorecards allow the organization's management team to define the number and to label the categories to fit the organization's current and future strategies.

Performance Scorecards thus allow greater flexibility for measurement categories, using category titles that reflect "key result areas" of organization-specific strategies and business goals. As an organization develops, links, and cascades scorecards, key result areas are reinforced, giving emphasis to top-level business strategies and performance results. In short, Performance Scorecards help managers translate strategies into measurable actions and meaningful business results.

We're anxious to hear about your personal experiences applying the methodology described in *Performance Scorecards: Measuring the Right Things in the Real World.* Please visit our Website at *www.richardchangassociates.com* to share your personal stories about how you have been applying the methodology on the job and to review examples from other readers, or e-mail your stories to *performancescorecards@rca4results.com.*

Wishing you success as you continue to improve your ability to measure the right things!

Richard Chang
Mark Morgan
March 2000

Acknowledgments

When we decided to write this book, we knew it had to be designed and written in a manner different from other books already on the market addressing the topic of performance measurement. We wanted to present the information in a practical and realistic manner that reflects the challenges faced on the job when trying to define the "right" measures. We also felt the market had need for a book that addressed the requirements of leaders at all levels of the organization, who are expected to define the appropriate measures to evaluate performance success.

Special thanks go to the following:

⇨ The entire team of highly skilled associates at Richard Chang Associates, Inc., for supporting our efforts throughout the book-development process. Our special thanks to Craig Holly, Jill Hennigan, Doug Dalziel, Joe Wilson, Dick Geisert, Pamela Wade, Denise Jeffrey, Melissa Zirretta, Rich Baisner, and Dena Putnam, who provided extra support by reviewing content, documenting information, designing graphics, and helping with a wide variety of logistics around marketing and completing this book.

⇨ The team of talented professionals at Jossey-Bass, Inc., for providing the editing, marketing, and production support needed to bring this book to publication. Special thanks to Susan Williams, our insightful editor, for balancing a variety of needs and development requirements throughout the manuscript development process; to Julianna Gustafson, Paula Goldstein, and Dawn Kilgore, for providing invaluable support in the design and production of the book; and to the publicity, sales, and marketing teams for putting this book into the hands of readers around the world who could benefit from defining the right measures to evaluate performance.

- ➪ The valued colleagues who contributed significant refinements to the story line used in the book, including: Kirk Chartier, Andrew Armstrong, Kim Janson, Ed Emig, Fred Henn, Gary Smith, Colleen Catallo, Pam Schmidt, and many others.
- ➪ The organizations and publications that we have cited as references, including: the Baldrige National Quality Program, APQC, Harvard Business Review, and Quality Progress.
- ➪ Our extended family of clients, business colleagues, and close friends, for challenging, supporting, and advocating the Richard Chang Associates, Inc., approach to designing, developing, and deploying organization-wide measurement systems.

Finally, thank you to the readers of this book for having the interest, willingness, and tenacity continually to define the right measures to evaluate performance success in the real world.

Introduction

Performance Scorecards allow your company to manage more successfully and achieve greater results by focusing on the "vital few" measures that matter to your customers, your employees, and your stakeholders. Scorecards support deployment of business strategies, provide visibility on process problems, and help ensure that customers' needs are met.

Organizations that effectively manage measures achieve superior business results. Numerous studies support this intuitive claim. Morgan and Schiemann (1999) state that "high-performing companies tend to be better at people management and measurement than other organizations" (p. 47). In a News Commentary in *Quality Progress* (1996), Steven Hronec, worldwide director of Arthur Andersen's performance measurement service, said that "a strategic performance measurement system can lead a company to make a quantum leap in performance" (p. 22). Citing successes from Southwest Airlines, ServiceMaster, and Taco Bell, Heskett, Jones, Loveman, Sasser, and Schlesinger (1994) state in the *Harvard Business Review* that "measures drive action when they are related in ways that provide managers with direction. Only if the individual measures are tied together into a comprehensive picture will the service-profit chain provide a foundation for unprecedented profit and growth" (p. 174).

Lingle and Schiemann (1996) compared business results from fifty-eight companies with balanced measurement systems to sixty-four companies with financially oriented measurement systems. They found that "the most significant conclusion from the research is that measurement plays a crucial role in translating strategy into results. In fact, we have found that organizations which are tops in their industry, stellar financial performers, and adept change leaders, distinguish themselves by the following characteristics: having agreed-upon measures that managers understand; balancing financial and nonfinancial measures; linking strategic measures to operational ones; updating their strategic scorecard regularly; and clearly communicating measures and progress to all employees" (p. 56). The authors conclude that businesses are more successful when the companies "realize their organizations are complex environments that require greater alignment and a balanced set of performance gauges" (p. 59).

In simplest terms, a Performance Scorecard is a set of business measures linked to business strategies and goals. A single scorecard is used at a specific level of an organization—an executive team, a vice president, a manager, or a work team—to monitor and manage a specific area of the business. Defining the measures for a single scorecard is typically straightforward and easily accomplished. Implementing, deploying, and linking Performance Scorecards throughout an organization are more difficult to do. These activities require management involvement and leadership to develop systems for gathering, reporting, and using scorecards consistently.

Performance Scorecards are not isolated; they are linked vertically and horizontally to other scorecards in an organization. Vertical linkages connect scorecards to organizational strategy and top-level goals. Vertical linkages provide feedback that keeps managers and work teams focused on strategic priorities and corporate aims.

Horizontal linkages connect customers' requirements to process results at work team levels. Cross-functional work teams use linked Performance Scorecards to see their process "end-to-end" and evaluate whether the supplier/customer hand-offs deliver the right outcomes for customers.

Using a mid-level manager's scorecard as an example, Figure 0.1 summarizes scorecard linkages:

⇨   Top-level business objectives defined in the executive strategic goals;
⇨   Process measures from a work group's efforts;
⇨   Customers' requirements and process outcomes; and
⇨   Suppliers' performance requirements.

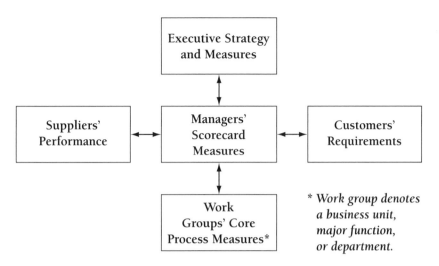

Figure 0.1. *Scorecards As a Link for Business Strategy*

Scorecards include charts and graphs that depict historical and/or projected performance of the key measures. Charts are used during management reviews to evaluate performance to targets, monitor trends, identify strengths and weaknesses, and provide feedback on management actions.

Developing scorecards involves a six-phase process:

⇨ Collect

⇨ Create

⇨ Cultivate

⇨ Cascade

⇨ Connect

⇨ Confirm

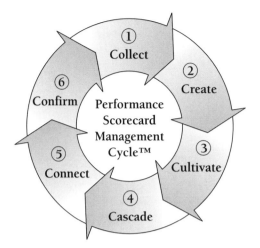

Figure 0.2. *The Performance Scorecard Management Cycle*

From these phases, you produce and deploy linked scorecards, providing results-oriented feedback that enables managers and work teams to focus time, attention, and resources on improved results.

The Performance Scorecard Management Cycle, illustrated in Figure 0.2, defines a simple six-phase approach that guides you through steps for building, linking, and refining scorecards.

PHASE 1: COLLECT

In the Collect Phase, you gather inputs for your Performance Scorecard from your organization's strategic goals and your senior-level measures and business objectives. Also, you identify your work teams' outcomes, core work processes, customers' expectations, and suppliers' requirements. Step-by-step instructions for the Collect Phase are given in Chapter 3.

PHASE 2: CREATE

Through scorecard development sessions, you and your management team create a scorecard, determining key result areas and associated measures. The key result areas are derived from your business strategies and are unique to your organization, but typically include areas similar to the following:

➪ Financial Success

➪ Customer Loyalty

➪ Market Leadership

➪ Employee Development

➪ Operational Effectiveness

➪ Community Impact

Also, you begin compiling the baseline for your scorecard measures and build momentum toward achieving your targets and goals. Steps for the Create Phase are explained in Chapter 4.

PHASE 3: CULTIVATE

During the Cultivate Phase, you conduct systematic reviews with your Performance Scorecard to monitor and improve business performance. You gather data and determine appropriate targets. Also, you refine objectives and measures to be more relevant and results-oriented. Actions for the Cultivate Phase are described in Chapter 5.

PHASE 4: CASCADE

Through the Cascade Phase, you strengthen links, improve visibility on business performance, and align efforts toward business goals at the front-line organizational level. In this phase, you establish work group scorecards and review your management scorecard for potential summary measures, as described in Chapter 6.

PHASE 5: CONNECT

During this phase, you connect objectives and measures to individual employees by developing individual performance plans, conducting one-on-one sessions with employees, and providing ongoing coaching. Employees relate their efforts to scorecard results and use feedback to drive improvements and outcomes toward business targets. Steps for the Connect Phase are described in Chapter 7.

PHASE 6: CONFIRM

In the Confirm Phase, you validate the effectiveness of your measures. In addition to assessing whether you have the right measures, you determine whether you have the right number of measures. You begin to understand how certain measures on your scorecard are related to one another and how to "pull the levers" to achieve desired outcomes. Chapter 8 provides details for evaluating your measures, processes for continually refining your Performance Scorecard, and tips for dealing with issues that surface as you develop better measures.

The amount of time it takes to complete all six phases depends on the size of your organization, the complexity of work processes in your group, your commitment, the maturity of your current measures, and the availability of data from your information systems. For organizations that have a vision, mission, and business goals already defined, the Collect and Create Phases take approximately two to four days. The remaining phases require ongoing actions to integrate improved measurement practices with normal business activities. Steady implementation over six to twelve months yields dramatic results and insights as to your true business performance. Ongoing application of the Performance Scorecard Management Cycle over successive years (see Figure 0.3 below) will continue to help improve organizational performance over time.

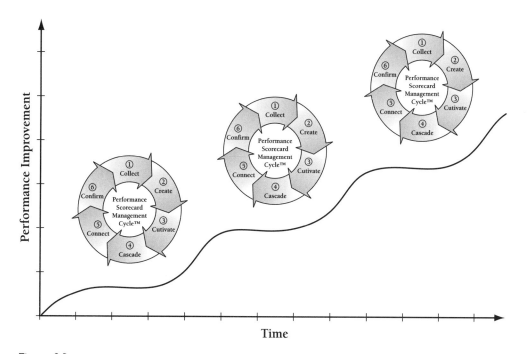

Figure 0.3. *Application of the Performance Scorecard Management Cycle over Time*

As you refine measures, you gain the advantage of more effective use of resources, better decisions, and greater insight to align work activities, eliminate waste, and achieve results. You don't need to complete all six phases before you realize results. As you proceed, you will:

➪ Identify opportunities and execute improvement actions;

➪ Help employees focus on business priorities and realize results;

➪ Clear out the clutter of obsolete or irrelevant measures;

➪ Improve your visibility on work processes and business outcomes;

➪ Understand relationships between measures and performance; and

➪ Gain an ability to predict performance changes based on common and special causes.

Scorecards work when the executive management team is involved in their development and use. The following should always be involved in scorecard development:

➪ The senior management team, as they must lead the effort and provide guidance, direction, and resources;

➪ Managers, staff specialists, and measurement personnel, as they support development and deployment of scorecards;

➪ Specialists within the business unit, as they support implementation and deployment; and

➪ Everyone else in your organization, as they use improved measures to deliver greater value and improved services to customers.

PERFORMANCE
SCORECARDS

CHAPTER 1

The Performance Problem

∙∙∙

"Why can't I make any sense of this?" Vince Sharp slammed the latest stack of operations reports down on his desk and hammered his fist on top of the stack. Vince, vice president of customer services for SolvNET, was furious because he suspected that service had dropped for the fourth straight month. He couldn't tell, though, because the reports were too complex to decipher.

Just then, Vince's new executive assistant, Libby Bates, stepped into his office to drop off the latest stack of customer feedback cards. Seeing the scattered reports and the scowl on Vince's face, Libby nearly tiptoed as she asked, "Having a rough day?"

"No more than usual," Vince replied. "We can't seem to generate any momentum toward our targets. Just when things seem to be moving in the right direction, we get a surprise. And, the surprises go on forever. It's crazy—and very frustrating."

Libby winced. "I'm not sure these customer feedback cards will brighten your day. Looks like there are more complaints than compliments in there."

Vince sighed. His frustration had been building for three months, ever since he had been personally selected and promoted by the SolvNET president, Jan Larson, to turn performance around in the Customer Services Department. He was very concerned about declining performance.

Vince had been the top sales representative from the Sales and Marketing Group, and

> ## SolvNET
>
> **(A fictitious company)**
>
> SolvNET is a division of the Performance Technologies Group, a $2-billion information technology organization that designs and develops networking hardware and software for a host of industries. SolvNET is a $100-million division of PTG, specializing in information services, including work station and network services support, software development, consulting, documentation, and training.

1

Jan expected Vince to achieve the same high performance with customer services. But his new team wasn't able to keep things moving forward consistently. He knew performance needed to improve—soon.

Vince's boss was impatient for improvements in service, expenses, customer satisfaction, and market growth. Vince struggled to convey the seriousness of the situation to his managers. They would get together over endless meetings and review countless reports, but nothing ever seemed to improve. On top of that, Vince felt that the customer services managers felt some resentment because he had been promoted into the group.

Vince looked at Libby with a weary expression: "How do other companies do it? How do they keep growing when it's this tough? We just downsized to cut expenses, but that increased the workload on remaining staff and drove up overtime costs. We're not satisfying many customers according to these cards. We know we're not meeting service goals, and I don't even know if we're making money because cost reports are always a month late. And, two more people resigned this week. They weren't happy because they didn't feel like they made a contribution."

Libby smiled sympathetically, "Gee, is that all?"

Vince smiled back, "Yeah, that's quite a load. But there's no time to manage because I spend all my time with paperwork. Look at these reports. This is way too much to absorb, but it's all my responsibility. I can't give up any of it."

"Who else sees these reports?" Libby asked.

"No one. I'm accountable for all these areas. The reports really wouldn't make sense to anyone else. They barely make sense to me," Vince answered.

Vince Sharp's Organization:

SolvNET Customer Services

Mission:

Provide premier information technology services and support to a variety of internal and external customers.

Customer Services' Departments:

- Help Desk
- Work Station Services
- Network Services
- Technology Integration

Libby pressed further: "What about your managers? What do they receive?"

Vince said, "Oh, I give them reports when we have a problem. We sit down and go through the numbers in great detail. Most of them are surprised when they see the results."

"Wow," Libby said, "you need Performance Scorecards."

"Scorecards?" Vince asked. "Libby, this is a business, not a bowling league."

"Oh, they're great for business," explained Libby. "My former company tracked results with scorecards. They were easy to understand and gave us the information we needed. We could quickly determine how we were doing compared to targets. Everyone could see where the problems were—and they didn't remain problems for long. Every department had a scorecard."

"What's on these scorecards?" Vince asked.

"A scorecard has graphs that summarize what you need to know—costs, customer satisfaction, employee satisfaction, service performance, sales—things you have to keep your eye on. It's all condensed in a page or two. If you need more information, you dig down to other scorecards," Libby explained.

Vince's interest was growing. "Does everyone have the same scorecard?"

"Oh, no," Libby said, "every manager and every work team has a unique scorecard. They're similar, but different."

Vince frowned, "Libby, you lost me there. How can they be similar but different?"

Libby didn't want her new boss to be upset.

SolvNET's Organization:

Mission:

Provide customer satisfaction through premier installation, repair, and upgrade services for computer networks, work stations, and associated systems.

Departments:

- Customer Services
- Software Development
- Engineering and Product Design
- Training and Documentation
- Consulting Services
- Sales and Marketing
- Administration

"Hang on, it's really very simple. It started with senior management's team scorecard. My boss reviewed it with me twice a year. It had about ten indicators, charts with company sales, expenses, market share, customer satisfaction, employee satisfaction, and things like that. The indicators were grouped in categories, like 'customer satisfaction,' 'financial fitness,' 'market growth,' 'employee development'—you know, the things that people care about in the business.

"My boss had a scorecard with the same categories as other vice presidents, but his indicators were different," Libby continued. "With his scorecard, he tracked his department's outcomes that related to the senior management scorecard. His scorecard had department sales, expenses, customer satisfaction ratings, and so on. I was responsible for preparing the scorecard from data furnished to me from other executive assistants and staff specialists. Also, I passed on some of the results for the senior management scorecard, but not all. Other vice presidents contributed their parts. All together, they added up to the executive scorecard."

Vince started to relax, "Let me see whether I understand how this works. If my boss has an expense target for the whole company, I track my share and Gene Ellis in sales and marketing has his own unique expense target that's tied to our boss's target. We each have our own expense measure on our scorecards."

Libby brightened visibly, "Right, that's exactly how it works. You do the same thing with indicators for sales, customer satisfaction, employee satisfaction—just about anything!"

Vince remained skeptical, "That's a wonderful theory, but I don't know if it will work here. We have so many measures it will be impossible to sort it all out. Where would we begin?"

Libby smiled, "Oh, it's a lot more than theory. It really works and it's the way they run the business at my former company. We learned that managing with scorecards forced us to be clear on what we were trying to accomplish and who was accountable for results. At first, people didn't like it because they thought it would result in more measures. As we got into it, we used fewer measures, while business results improved. Eventually, scorecards were the norm because we knew what to watch and when to take action. We realized less time was wasted reviewing reports and analyzing problems. We knew where the problems were, and we knew whether things were getting better. Getting through it wasn't that hard, once we made the commitment."

"OK, you've got my curiosity up. What was involved in 'getting through it'?" Vince asked.

Libby paused, "Wow, you're serious about this. Tell you what—I'll dig out my notes and scorecard examples and show you how we did it. I think you'll be amazed by its simplicity. But putting it all together took a fair amount of commitment and effort from senior managers. I'll admit that they struggled for a while until it started coming together."

It was Vince's turn to smile, "Anything is better than what we have now—a lot of numbers that don't tell me anything. I'm very interested in learning how your company did it. How long will it take to find your notes?"

Libby thought for a moment, "I know where I put them at home. I'll pull them out tonight, and we can go through them tomorrow. It looks like you have an hour open from 10 to 11 tomorrow morning. Should we go through the notes then?"

Vince's mood brightened. "That sounds great. Libby, you're a godsend for your ideas on scorecards," he said. "I can't wait to learn more."

Measurement Case Study: The Ritz-Carlton Hotel Company

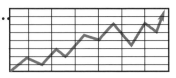

The Ritz-Carlton, the premier name in the hospitality industry, won the Malcolm Baldrige National Quality Award in 1992. This milestone and continued growth were achieved from The Ritz-Carlton's use of a scorecard approach to measurement. Specifically, it uses a set of measures from different performance categories to analyze the overall health of the organization. Fifty percent of its measures are standard marketing and financial data, and 50 percent are measures related to customers, employees, and quality operations.

They take to heart one of the fundamental principles of Performance Scorecards—to focus attention on a vital few measures. Their philosophy: We only measure what we must, but we make sure that what we measure is important to our customers.

As a foundation for the scorecard, The Ritz-Carlton goes out of its way to collect customer information. Key customer requirements are determined through extensive customer surveys and focus groups. The Ritz-Carlton discovered that people don't always express what they really want. To remedy this, the hotel performs a language analysis on customer responses in focus groups. They not only ask questions, but also use experts to interpret what customers really mean.

Customers' needs become the basis of operational measures that include guest room preventive maintenance cycles per year, percentage of check-ins with no queuing, time spent to achieve industry-best clean room appearance, and time to service an occupied guest room.

Results of the hotel's measures are reported daily and monitored for trends monthly, quarterly, and annually. The Ritz-Carlton uses daily quality production reports to determine if a problem needs to be immediately addressed. Data submitted from each work area serve as an early warning system for identifying problems that can impede progress toward meeting quality and customer satisfaction goals. Together with quarterly summaries of guest reactions, combined results are compared with predetermined customer expectations to continually improve services.

The aim of these and other customer-focused measures is to provide guests with a "memorable visit." Judging from surveys conducted by an independent research firm, 92 to 97 percent of the company's guests leave with that impression. Coupled with 121 quality awards within the last decade and industry-best rankings by all three major hotel-rating organizations, The Ritz-Carlton demonstrates the power and purpose of measuring the right things.

"Measuring for Excellence" by Laura Struebing. *Quality Progress* (December 1996). Milwaukee, WI: American Society for Quality. Copyright © 1996 American Society for Quality. Reprinted with Permission.

Baldrige National Quality Program (1999). *Malcolm Baldrige National Quality Award: Profiles of Winners.* Gaithersburg, MD: National Institute of Standards and Technology.

CHAPTER 2

Setting the Stage for Scorecards

In this chapter, Libby explains the concept of scorecards to Vince and provides a few examples used by her previous employer. She shows Vince the steps her former company went through to develop Performance Scorecards. The chapter concludes with Vince meeting a business consultant to discover more insights to scorecard development and drawing up an action plan to begin.

The next day, Libby returned to work with her notes on Performance Scorecards. At the stroke of 10 a.m., she walked into Vince's office. Vince was finishing a telephone call and motioned Libby to a small conference table. Vince completed his call and joined Libby at the table.

"I hope you're here to solve all of our performance problems," Vince said wryly. "That was Jan Larson asking about our sales and expenses. I need some quick answers."

"I can't promise immediate answers, but these ideas will help," Libby responded. "I pulled out a few old scorecards that I saved and my notes from our efforts to create them. I think you'll like what's here."

"Great, let's start with the basics. Help me understand again. Just what is a scorecard?" Vince asked.

> **Expert Tip**
>
> A Performance Scorecard is a selected set of measures that provides a balanced and timely view of business performance specific to an area of responsibility.

Libby replied, "I've forgotten the official definition, but I would define a scorecard as a concise set of measures that you regularly use to evaluate and manage your business. The scorecard includes measurement information, usually in visual chart form, with trends, targets, and benchmarks."

Vince nodded, "OK, that makes sense. What were you saying yesterday about everyone having unique scorecards? How do we run the business if everyone is looking at different measures?"

"Each manager's scorecard is unique, but there are similar categories and measures on all managers' scorecards. It's easy when you realize scorecards are linked," Libby said.

"Linked scorecards?" Vince asked. "How does that work?"

Libby explained, "I'm not sure how it might work at SolvNET yet, but at my former company we knew that everyone in our business had some part in the service chain that led to customers. We called it the 'value chain.'"

"Sure," Vince agreed, "we looked at our work processes a month ago and traced the value chain of a service order through our departments. We learned how many departments handle a service order from a customer request to service delivery. But what does that have to do with scorecards?"

"That's where the unique and linked features of scorecards come in," Libby explained. "Because every manager owns a part of the overall process, that person's scorecard reflects his or her part. Just as the parts of the process are linked to complete the service order, the scorecards are linked to reflect the entire process."

"This is starting to make sense, Libby. Let me give you an example to see if I understand," Vince said.

"Sure," Libby encouraged him.

Vince said, "As vice president of customer services for SolvNET, I track customer satisfaction, but customer satisfaction is partially based on Gene Ellis' people in sales and marketing, who have to input orders correctly. My service specialists can't satisfy a customer if they can't find the customer when sales records the wrong address.

"Ideally," Vince continued, "I would have a measure of customer satisfaction from feedback cards on my scorecard that shows satisfaction from my service technicians. Gene Ellis over in sales and marketing has a customer satisfaction measure from his part of the order-taking process. Together, we provide an overall customer satisfaction rating."

"Right," Libby agreed, "because both of you report to the SolvNET president, Jan Larson, Jan will have an overall measure of customer satisfaction based on order taking and service delivery. So, scorecards are unique, yet linked."

"That's fantastic!" Vince exclaimed. "That way Jan gets a view of overall customer satisfaction, while Gene and I get visibility on the part we own. If overall satisfaction goes down, we see it and know where to treat the problem. Because we're peers across the process, that sounds like horizontal linkage. Is there such a thing as vertical linkage?"

"Sure," Libby said. "Vertical linkage connects scorecards with the vision, mission, and strategic goals of the business. That way, everyone knows the important categories and items to measure. The vertical linkage extends all the way from Jan Larson to front-line service teams of SolvNET."

"Whoa," Vince exclaimed, "did I just hear you say that Jan will have the same measures as my service specialists?"

"No," Libby said, "their measures are related, but different. For example, Jan, as SolvNET president, is interested in overall service to customers. But she can't possibly watch all aspects of service quality. So, your service specialists will have a measure specific to their work, such as response time or fixing problems the first time. Jan will have a summary measure for service quality that includes measures from your service specialists and measures from service ordering, software development, engineering, the help desk, and other areas."

"Sounds like a lot to put together," Vince said. "I'd like to keep this simple."

Libby said, "It is a simple way to manage when it's all put together, but assembling the pieces takes some time—sort of like a jigsaw puzzle. At first, the pieces don't appear to fit together, but once you build the frame and start filling in the pieces, an entirely different picture emerges."

"Could you give me an example of what it looks like when it comes together into a scorecard?" Vince said.

"Here's an example from my former company. Take a look," Libby said.

Vince looked at Libby's example, shown in Figure 2.1.

"This looks pretty good," Vince said. "That's a lot of information. How did you learn to set this up?"

"We had help from a business consultant, Bob Kelly. He's very good, and I know he could help us. Want me to call him?"

"Absolutely," Vince replied. "I would love to talk with him about how this works. Can you arrange something?"

Libby nodded, "I'd be glad to call him. I'll check your schedule and arrange a meeting."

"I'll look forward to meeting Bob—soon. We need to move quickly on this, because Jan Larson has high expectations to turn our performance around. Libby, thanks for bringing this to my attention. Let's look through the rest of your notes to see what I might need to know for our meeting," Vince said. Libby and Vince continued for the remainder of the hour discussing Performance Scorecards.

Later that day, Libby contacted Bob Kelly, who was delighted to meet with Vince. Two days later, Bob and Libby met in Vince's office at 3 p.m. After getting acquainted, Vince jumped right into his questions on Performance Scorecards.

"Libby's done a great job of explaining this so far, but all this linking and measuring sounds like a lot of work," Vince commented.

"It takes effort, but it's worth it," Bob said. "Every management team we've worked with is very happy with the results and with the ability scorecards provide to see and manage performance more easily. Scorecards ensure that work teams are connected in the right ways both to run operations efficiently and to deliver customer

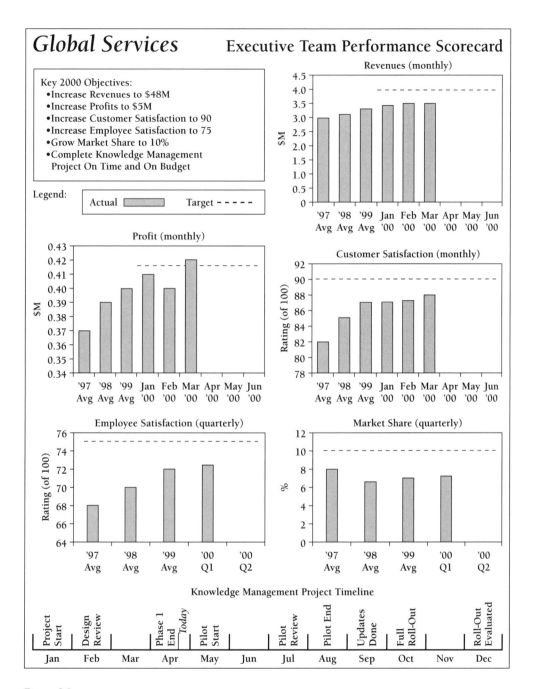

Figure 2.1. *Sample Executive Team Performance Scorecard*

value effectively. With better measures aligning team efforts, redundancies and problems disappear, resulting in greater productivity and lower costs."

"Sounds too good to be true," Vince said.

"We thought that, too, at first," Bob chuckled. "But we found several studies that convinced us that good measures are the heart of managing a company effectively."

"What type of studies?" Vince asked.

Bob pulled a notebook out of his briefcase. "Here are some highlights of studies from the American Productivity and Quality Center, the American Society for Quality, the *Harvard Business Review*, the American Management Association, and profiles of the winners of the United States Malcolm Baldrige National Quality Award. They all show quantifiable improvements in business results from having better business measures."

Vince spent a few minutes scanning the studies and was impressed. "So, scorecards and measures make a big difference. I didn't realize the results were so dramatic."

"Sure, there are a lot of studies and success stories that back up these findings," Bob said. "Of course, scorecards must be relevant for your business. You can't copy someone else's scorecard or just track a few random measures and expect all the right things to happen."

Bob, Libby, and Vince continued their conversation well into the evening. Vince was filled with questions about how to proceed, and Bob and Libby were delighted to share their knowledge and experience. Bob shared with Vince a sample scorecard and the six-step process to develop scorecards. Bob explained the roles of various individuals for developing scorecards.

Vince felt that Bob's expertise would be invaluable, and they reached an agreement for continuing Bob's services as a consultant on the project. Vince was eager to get started, but remained concerned about the investment of time and the need for immediate results.

"This is terrific, Bob, but now the big question: Where do we start?" Vince asked.

"Start at the beginning—Phase 1," Bob said. "You need to *collect inputs* and plan a *scorecard development meeting*. Your scorecard has to align with company strategy and business goals, so you need to pull it all together."

"Do you have a summary list that will help me pull it together?" Vince asked.

"I'll send you an e-mail that lists what you'll need to collect and how to prepare for the meeting. Would that be all right?" Bob said.

With Vince's "Yes," Bob, Vince, and Libby concluded their meeting with Vince's thanks to Bob and Libby for all the information. As Bob left, Vince thought this might be just what he needed to sort out his data and get his team on track.

Summary

Performance Scorecards provide measures that allow you and your work team to focus attention on the vital few measures for success. By linking scorecards, your business gains a competitive advantage by clarifying outcomes, improving end-to-end visibility of work processes, and eliminating the time and expense of tracking irrelevant information.

There are six phases for developing and using scorecards to manage performance: *Collect, Create, Cultivate, Cascade, Connect,* and *Confirm.* Applying the steps yields scorecards that are specific and relevant to work teams and linked vertically and horizontally across the organization. This provides managers and work teams feedback on key measures that align efforts toward business objectives while strengthening the overall fabric of the organization.

Measurement Case Study: Wainwright Industries

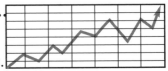

Wainwright Industries is no stranger to awards. Based in St. Peters, Missouri, the company won the 1994 Malcolm Baldrige National Quality Award and the 1999 Missouri Industry of the Year Award. The company's rise to national recognition is due largely to a rigorous set of measurements and processes that align all critical operations.

Wainwright Industries manufactures high-precision stampings and assemblies for the automobile and aerospace industries. Their vision states a "continuous commitment to our customers' future."

To turn their vision into reality, a work area they've named "Mission Control" is the hub for measuring operational performance. CEO Don Wainwright explains that they have "created a visual scheme for displaying the information that allows anyone to walk in and take the pulse of the company in a heartbeat."

Five key indicators are on display at Mission Control to measure the company's overall performance:

1. *Safety.* There is a genuine concern about the well-being of their associates. When associates are focused on safety, there is a natural inclination to look for and find other opportunities for improvement. The numbers speak for themselves. Wainwright Industries reported a nine-fold reduction in Workers' Compensation claims, enough to earn safety awards from the Liberty Mutual Insurance Company and the Missouri Division of Workers' Compensation.

2. *Internal Customer Satisfaction Index (ICSI).* Associates focus on internal customer relationships as well as external relationships. They measure their satisfaction with their supervisors and supporting departments. For example, a manager's performance is rated by his or her employees.

3. *External Customer Satisfaction Index (ECSI).* Data from the monthly report cards for all customers are combined into a single number each month. This represents the overall customer satisfaction level.

4. *Six-Sigma Quality.* Defect rates are measured in parts per million (PPM). The long-term goal is to reach six sigma (3.4 PPM). They've already exceeded that goal with some customers. One customer received over twenty million parts during a three-year span without a single defect.

5. *Business Performance.* This is the key measure of financial performance. A core belief at Wainwright Industries is that when the first four indicators are on target, financial results will follow. The trend has supported the belief. Gross margins improved by 35 percent in three years. Other improvements were noted for debt reduction, market share, sales, and net income.

Wainwright receives monthly report cards from its customers. Grades are translated into numerical equivalents: A = 100, B = 90, C = 50, and D = 0. A grade of B or lower requires a corrective action plan within 24 hours. A team that includes management, a customer liaison, and customer representatives meets to analyze the problem, develop the corrective action plan, and ensure problem resolution and closure.

The walls of Mission Control are plastered with red and green pennants, status reports, and charts. A green pennant indicates that Wainwright is meeting targets. A red pennant indicates a potential or real problem. Not surprisingly, most of the pennants are green. Don Wainwright explains that short-term results aren't as important as the trend: "We want the results, but we emphasize the long view. Culture takes time to change, so if the trend lines are sloping in the right direction, we know the results will follow. That's really the essence of continuous improvement."

"Leading the Duck at Mission Control" by Les Landes. *Quality Progress* (July 1995). Milwaukee, WI: American Society for Quality. Copyright © 1995 American Society for Quality. Reprinted with Permission.

Baldrige National Quality Program (1999). *Malcolm Baldrige National Quality Award: Profiles of Winners.* Gaithersburg, MD: National Institute of Standards and Technology.

CHAPTER 3

Collect Scorecard Inputs

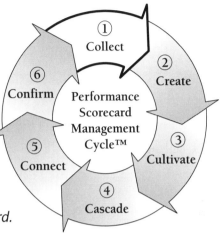

In this chapter, Libby and Bob help Vince through the first phase of developing Vince's Performance Scorecard. They walk Vince through the steps of compiling inputs and preparing for a staff meeting to create his initial scorecard. They advise him of issues he's likely to encounter and encourage him to continue despite some known obstacles. The chapter concludes with Vince preparing for an upcoming meeting with his staff to create the initial scorecard.

The next day, Vince was excited as he scanned his e-mail and found Bob's message. Vince's excitement evaporated as he reviewed Bob's list of items to collect:

1. Customers' key requirements;
2. Company vision, mission, strategic goals, and values;
3. Your boss's objectives, measures, and targets;
4. Your department's objectives, measures, and targets;
5. High-level core process flow charts; and
6. Existing measurement data for core business processes.

Collect

Steps

1. Obtain Top-Level Objectives, Measures, and Targets (i.e., the Boss's Scorecard)
2. Identify Customers and Key Requirements
3. Define Core Process Chains
4. Document High-Level Process Flows
5. Gather Existing Measurement Data
6. Plan the Scorecard Development Session and Agenda

Immediately, Vince called Bob on the phone and said, "Hey, Bob, thanks for your message and the list. But I'm more than surprised. Do I really need all of this? I thought this was about measurement!"

Bob said (chuckling), "Yes, it is a lot. But if you want to save time and money later, you're better off gathering these up front. You want to make sure you track the right measures. The only way is to start with your strategies, process flows, and customers' requirements."

"Why is all of that important?" Vince asked, "What happens if I don't have one of the things on the list?"

Bob replied, "While you can create a scorecard without everything, missing an item will make it more difficult to define and align your scorecard. All of the items are important because they are all connected. You begin with requirements for the customers you now serve, plus requirements of customers in markets you want to grow. Your strategies must align with customers' needs and expectations. For example, because you provide computer services, you probably have strategies for being quick and responsive."

Vince agreed, "Sure, and we like to distinguish ourselves by being professional and cost-effective. I'm with you so far."

Bob said, "Your business strategies define what you should measure. So, if you want to be quick, responsive, professional, and cost-effective, you have to measure those characteristics. Otherwise, how do you know whether you're good—or getting better?"

"OK, that makes sense." Vince said, "What about the core processes and flows?"

Bob answered, "Your core processes are the main work flows that deliver primary services to your customers. I'm sure you have

> **✎ Expert Tip**
>
> Collect outcomes include:
> - A "snapshot" of your customer-supplier process chains
> - High-level flow charts of core processes
> - Inputs and agenda for Scorecard Development Sessions

processes for receiving customer calls, responding to trouble calls, and installing new computer work stations."

Vince said, "Sure, along with processes for providing system administration services, distributing software, and troubleshooting network problems. All those are on flow charts."

"Are you measuring those areas now?" Bob asked.

Vince replied, "No, not as well as we should."

"That's why you need the information during the Collect Phase." Bob explained fur-

Collect

Step 1

Obtain Top-Level Objectives, Measures, and Targets

ther, "You need to sort through everything to identify the 'vital few' measures. So, you need your strategies, your process flows, and existing measurement data."

"I can see that all this is needed. So once I find all the information, what do I do?" Vince asked.

"That's the fun part," Bob said. "You arrange a session with your managers to review the information and create your scorecard. After that, they create their own scorecards."

"How does that work?" Vince wanted to know more. "That's a lot of information for one big group."

Bob said, "Sure it is, but that's the essential part of developing your scorecard. Tell you what, you get it all together and we'll meet again. I'll look it over and give you some pointers on what to look for and what to do. If you like, I'll facilitate the session for you."

"Yes, I'd like you to facilitate for us," Vince replied. "That should save us time and put us on the right track quickly. Could you and I meet tomorrow to move this along? I want to be ready before the regular staff meeting on Wednesday."

"Tomorrow afternoon sounds good," Bob said. "We need about three hours to go through your information and arrange an agenda to create the scorecard."

As Vince and Bob concluded their call, Vince began thinking about how his business strategies, objectives, customer requirements, process flows, and measures needed to fit together. He still didn't see it, but he was convinced that Bob was right—they had to fit for the measures to make sense. Intuitively, he felt his current measures were ineffective because they weren't linked to strategies.

Jan Larson, SolvNET's president, had provided Vince the company's vision, mission, and strategic goals when he'd been promoted to vice president of customer services. Up to this point, Vince had considered them an academic exercise that didn't mean much to his daily work. He reviewed them for the first time in three months.

SolvNET's VISION	To be the customer's first choice for information services throughout all of our service territories.
SolvNET's MISSION	We provide total customer satisfaction through premier installation, repair, and upgrade services for computer networks, work stations, and associated systems.
SolvNET's STRATEGIC GOALS	⇨ Build customer loyalty with each transaction ⇨ Grow profitably ⇨ Develop lean and efficient work systems ⇨ Achieve a competitive advantage with employee knowledge, skills, and capabilities

SolvNET's VALUES	⇨ Attentiveness to cost and value
	⇨ Profitability
	⇨ Pride in fulfilling our commitments
	⇨ Leadership in our industry
	⇨ Enjoyment of our work
	⇨ Sustained long-term growth

Vince reflected on these for a moment. He considered them important, but difficult to reinforce every day with all the details and problems that always came up. Still, he pressed on. He looked at SolvNET's business objectives for the current year.

SolvNET's BUSINESS OBJECTIVES for Current Year	By the end of the year:
	⇨ Increase revenues
	⇨ Increase profits
	⇨ Improve customer satisfaction
	⇨ Expand markets
	⇨ Improve service performance

For the first time, Vince noticed a discrepancy between some of the strategies and the business objectives. Specifically, he noted that the strategic goals and values associated with employee skills and capabilities were not related to any of the current objectives. He also noticed that no targets were provided with the goals and that the measures were implied.

> **Expert Tip**
>
> Effective scorecards depend on the clear alignment of measures from one level to the next. This vertical linkage of measures begins with your organization's vision, mission, and strategic goals.

Next, Vince dug through his files and located a study completed six months ago that analyzed customer feedback. The study gathered feedback for three key questions:

➪ What do customers expect from SolvNET?

➪ Are customers satisfied with the services provided by SolvNET?

➪ What major gaps exist between expectations and current service levels?

Vince remembered the study well, because he and his former sales team took some flak from the findings. Customers were clear on their expectations:

➪ No system or work station outages;

➪ Immediate responses when troubles occur;

➪ Knowledgeable, courteous, and efficient service specialists;

➪ Systems that match company requirements; and

➪ Competitive costs and service value.

Collect

Step 2

Identify Customers and Key Requirements

Vince remembered arguing with the former vice president of customer services about the requirements. The former VP had argued that customers' demands were unreasonable. Systems were always prone to fail at some point, so how could customers expect no outages? How could the customer services team provide immediate response when some customers were several miles from the service center? The VP thought he had a top-notch team that was knowledgeable, courteous, and efficient, but how could he balance keeping top-notch people and holding prices down? Did customers think good people worked for free?

Vince chuckled to himself, as he now owned the responsibility of fulfilling these "impossible" requirements. As he continued working through Bob's list, Vince paused at "Core Process Chain High-Level Flow." He was aware that customer services had completed a study of work processes a few months before he joined the group, and Vince remembered that the team struggled with the outcomes. They identified a few problems and worked on them, but they didn't provide the type of results everyone at SolvNET expected.

He located the study in the file drawer and found the section that identified the team's work processes:

- Managing Service Calls
- Repairing Work Stations
- Repairing Network Problems
- Maintaining Network Performance
- Maintaining Parts Inventory
- Providing Systems Administration
- Installing Work Stations

<table>
<tr><td>

Collect

Step 3

Define Core Process Chains

</td></tr>
</table>

The study provided endless details on the various process flows. Vince recalled the team's frustration over the amount of work they put into the flow charting and their confusion over what to do with the information. He hoped his next visit with Bob would help explain how all this information related to scorecards.

Finally, Vince added his own stack of management reports to the pile of information Bob had suggested. He laughed out loud when he thought how Bob would react to all the information on system outages, trouble calls, expenses, employee sick days, sales, and the host of details that Vince regularly reviewed. He couldn't wait for his next meeting with Bob.

For the rest of the day, Vince wondered how Bob would sort through all this information. Vince couldn't imagine having his entire team review the stack of reports. It was too overwhelming.

The next afternoon, Libby showed Bob into Vince's office. After a warm welcome, Vince pointed to the mound of information on his conference table. "Where do we start?" Vince asked.

"At the beginning," Bob answered. "Where in that pile are your company's vision, mission, and business goals?"

Vince helped Bob sort through the information for more than an hour. Bob asked questions about the study on customers' requirements and about the process flows, but did not seem the least bit concerned over what he found. In fact, Vince's anxiety increased as Bob became more relaxed.

"Good, it's all here," Bob said finally.

Vince smiled, "I hope so. It's more information than I thought we could ever use."

Bob smiled. "Exactly—that's part of the problem. You really have more measurement information than you need. But it all fits together. Let me show you."

Bob sketched the diagram shown in Figure 3.1. "Think of it all fitting together in a large pyramid," Bob explained. "The customers are at the top. Without them, you don't have a business. So you have to be very aware of their needs and expectations."

Figure 3.1. *Scorecard Measures Aligned with Customers' Needs and Expectations, Corporate Vision, and Business Processes*

Bob continued, "Your company's strategies and objectives need to match customers' needs. I see your company has vision and mission statements that are oriented toward customers. So far, so good."

"The next level down are your core processes," Bob said. "You've identified core processes in your area of responsibility, but I'm sure that your company has other work processes. This includes financial processes for billing customers, paying vendors, budgeting, and so on. And you must have processes for business planning, managing facilities, and others."

Collect

Step 4

Document High-Level Process Chains

Vince rolled his eyes, "If you can call them processes. Sometimes I wonder how work really gets done around here."

Bob smiled, "That's a typical observation from a company that doesn't manage with scorecards. Next, you have the measures from those processes."

"But we have all those. How are scorecards going to help us?"

"How many measures do you now track, Vince?" Bob asked.

Vince thought for a moment, "I never added them up, but I'd have to say hundreds."

"What if I told you that you should watch fewer than twenty measures?"

"Twenty!" Vince cried. "There's no way. I can't let the others fall off. And they would if I didn't watch all of them."

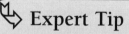

Expert Tip

A "core process" is the sequence of work activities that provides goods and/or services to customers.

"I'm not saying all of the hundreds shouldn't be watched," Bob said. "I'm only suggesting that you don't have to be the one to watch all of them. Actually, if they are linked properly, you can watch the hundreds with fewer than twenty. But we'll come to that later." Bob explained, "As a vice president, you need to be concerned with answers to seven primary questions for your business.

1. What does it cost to operate?

2. What revenues and profits are generated?

3. How long does it take to perform or complete a service order?

4. How much work volume is completed?

5. How many resources are used? (This should include labor, materials, capital, and consumables.)

6. How many defects are generated in the form of mistakes, rework, scrap, and waste?

7. How satisfied are customers with the outputs?

Do you know that information from these reports?"

Vince looked uncertain, "I'm not sure. I would have to say no."

Bob smiled, "With scorecards, Vince, there's no guessing. You have the information in front of you for those seven measures, plus others that you consider important, such as employee satisfaction, employee skill development, or market conditions."

> **Collect**
>
> **Step 5**
>
> Gather Existing Measurement Data

"What happens with all the information in these reports?" Vince asked.

Bob replied, "Many of these measures appear to be lower-level indicators that tie to your view of the seven summary measures I mentioned. The lower-level indicators are monitored at supervisor and work-team levels. Your managers and directors review roll-up measures, and you review summary measures. If the measures are linked, you drill down to lower-level indicators when needed."

"That's what Libby said," Vince said. "Can you give me an example from this data?"

"Sure," Bob said, "look at all this data on system outages."

"I have to keep a close eye on that," Vince said. "Customers raise a royal stink when outages occur."

"But who fixes the outages—or works to prevent outages? Is that your job, Vince?" Bob asked.

"Of course not; my network techs do that," Vince said.

"Do your network techs review system outage data?" Bob asked.

"I don't know. I think so," Vince said.

"There you go again, guessing, " Bob said. "With linked scorecards, your network techs review system outage data daily to see where problems occur and look for ways to prevent outages. You review outage data for all systems weekly, possibly monthly, looking for long-term trends. You want to put the feedback in the hands of people who can use the data—in this case, your network techs."

"So, I don't get rid of the data, I just push it down to the right level and make others responsible to monitor the results?" Vince mused.

"Generally speaking, that's right," Bob said.

"Sounds good, but how do I sort through all of this to determine who should own all of the different pieces—and how they link together?" Vince asked.

"Start with your staff and bring them together for a scorecard development session," Bob

---

Collect

Step 6

Plan the Scorecard Development Session and Agenda

---

explained, "where you and key members of your team create your scorecard measures related to your business objectives, targets, and plans. If you haven't defined your business objectives, this is an ideal opportunity to discuss and refine them."

"Oh, we've discussed our objectives," Vince said. "That's the problem—no one's meeting them."

"That could be because they aren't sure what to measure or because they don't have enough feedback to know what's happening," Bob mused. "Get your direct reports together, along with staff members who compile your measures, such as your process managers or performance improvement specialists. Since your team is aware of your business goals, you should schedule a half-day meeting to review and refine measures leading to your scorecard. As you coordinate meeting arrangements, provide advance copies of the input you gathered from the Collect Phase. This will save meeting time and help participants prepare for the session."

"That's a lot of information for them to review. What would the agenda look like to accomplish that in only half a day?" Vince asked.

"I was hoping we'd get to that point, so I brought a sample," Bob said. "You'll want to tailor the agenda to your business and your audience, but this gives you an idea. Take a look." Bob's example is shown in Figure 3.2.

"If you can help us accomplish all of that in half a day, I would really like you to facilitate the session. I think scorecards will help us, and I'm ready to move with this. Can you be here Wednesday?" Vince asked.

Bob said, "Absolutely, I'm happy to help you get started. Let's spend a minute tailoring this agenda to your specific team. Also, I need to explain what happens after the session. This session is only to define your measures. You need to develop baselines, use your scorecards, and drive improvements. There's plenty of work ahead."

"Well, then, we'd better get started," Vince responded.

Vince and Bob spent another two hours refining the agenda for Vince's team and preparing for the session. After Bob left, Vince notified his four managers and one staff specialist about the upcoming meeting. As he finished the day, he took one more look at the stack on his conference table. He would be very happy to make it go away.

TIME	CONTENT	PROCESS	PROCESS LEAD(S)	TOOLS/ RESOURCES
0.5 hour	OPENING • Welcome • Desired session outcomes • Overview of Scorecard Development Methodology	• Information Sharing • Q & A	• Team Leader • Scorecard Development Facilitator	• Session Agenda • Scorecard Development Process Model • Rationale for developing a scorecard and improving performance measures
0.5 hour	REVIEW COMPANY INPUTS	• Information Sharing • Q & A	• Team Leader • Scorecard Development Facilitator	• Organization Mission and Vision • Senior Management's Scorecard • Immediate Manager's Scorecard
0.5 hour	REVIEW CORE PROCESSES AND OBJECTIVES	• Discussion • Q & A • Planning Activity	• Scorecard Development Facilitator	• Core Process Flows • Team Outputs • Customer Requirements • Team Business Objectives
1.5 hours	DEVELOP INITIAL SCORECARD MEASURES	• Discussion • Group Activity	• Scorecard Development Facilitator	• Worksheet: *Developing Measures*

Figure 3.2. *Sample Agenda for a Scorecard Development Session*

TIME	CONTENT	PROCESS	PROCESS LEAD(S)	TOOLS/ RESOURCES
0.5 hour	DEVELOP ACTION PLANS	• Discussion • Planning	• Scorecard Development Facilitator	• Worksheet: *Action Planning*
1 hour	WRAP-UP/NEXT STEPS • Discuss Next Steps • Review Action Items • Set the Stage for Phase 3: Cultivate Your Scorecard	• Discussion • Report Next Steps	• Team Leader • Scorecard Development Facilitator	• Action Summary • Agenda Planning

Figure 3.2. *Continued*

Summary

There are six steps to the Collect Phase, summarized with the outcomes in the chart that follows. During the Collect Phase, you review and analyze scorecard inputs, including business objectives and higher-level measures. Also, you define the customer-supplier chain specific to your organization and develop high-level flow charts of your core processes. Additionally, you define your team objectives and desired outcomes.

This information is the framework for the scorecard development session, during which you define your scorecard measures and create your initial scorecard. This ensures that your scorecard measures will match your organization's strategic aims, your customers' requirements, and your work unit's business objectives.

PHASE	STEPS	OUTCOMES

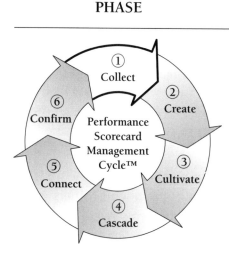

Phase 1: COLLECT

1. Obtain top-level objectives, measures, and targets (i.e., the boss's score-card).

2. Identify customers and key requirements.

3. Define core process chains.

4. Document high-level process flows.

5. Gather existing measurement data.

6. Plan the score-card development session and agenda.

- A snapshot of your customer-supplier process chain

- High-level flow charts of core processes

- Inputs and agenda for scorecard development sessions

Measurement Case Study: Granite Rock Company

An APQC Measurement Case Study

The family-owned Granite Rock Company started nearly one hundred years ago, and there is ample evidence that their past successes will reach well into the next century. In 1992, to punctuate a relentless attention to measurement, the company became the first construction firm to win the Malcolm Baldrige National Quality Award.

Granite Rock Company initiated its measurement program not in the midst of a crisis, but during a time of financial success. In 1986 when brothers Bruce and Steve Woolpert took over as joint CEOs, they became aware that there were no corporate goals other than improving the bottom line in current use. Additionally, there were no metrics to gauge progress.

Their efforts to remake Granite Rock Company began with identification of nine objectives, strategic areas of key importance to the company. These became the main categories for measures and include the following:

1. Customer Satisfaction and Service
2. Safety
3. Production Efficiency
4. Financial Performance and Growth
5. Community Commitment
6. Management
7. Profit
8. Product Quality Assurance
9. People

Next, they established four or five baseline metrics or measures for each result area. They used three approaches to define metrics:

⇨ Surveys and focus groups to find out what was important to their customers and Granite Rock people;

⇨   Benchmarking studies inside and outside of their industry; and

⇨   Internally defined measures based on their customers' expectation of value.

Knowing that measurement drives behavior, they used measures to improve competitiveness. For example, they aimed to improve "production efficiency," which lowers costs and makes them more competitive. If they are price competitive and offer higher value, customers buy more. So, within the production efficiency area, they have four or five metrics that focus employees on efficiency and product quality, balancing production, quality, and costs.

The company divisions decide which metrics are important for them to match to the advancement of corporate objectives. For example, the division sales manager from the Northern Road Materials Division measures customer satisfaction through "gate-to-gate" time (that is, the amount of time a truck spends in the asphalt plant before getting on the road again), saving customers truck time and money.

These division measures link to corporate objectives. Relating management compensation with measurement results rewards performance. Also, Granite Rock makes a point of sharing measurement results with everyone. In a clever play on words, their newsletter, *Tuesday Facts,* is faxed and sent electronically over the company's intranet from the corporate office to the branches each Tuesday.

In the aftermath of winning the Baldrige Award, Granite Rock has experienced numerous achievements, including:

⇨   Sales improved more than 25 percent, with an increase in the total number of customers of more than 25 percent;

⇨   Market share has increased every year since 1992;

⇨   Customer satisfaction, as indicated by scores on the company's customer satisfaction survey, jumped from 4.29 out of a possible 5 to 4.65;

⇨   Statistical Process Control (SPC) has improved concrete batching consistency by more than 100 percent;

⇨   The company has earned numerous environmental awards and an innovation award;

- They received the California Governor's Golden State Quality Award in 1994; and

- Cycle time for Product Service Discrepancy (PSD) investigations (for resolving customer complaints) has dropped from 23 days to six days. The total PSD process completion time has dropped from 60 days to 29 days.

In leading its industry, Granite Rock understands that continuous improvement through measurement is *not an option, but a requirement.*

"Measuring Success: Winning the Baldrige Was Just a Step Along Granite Rock's Endless Road to Quality," by Susan Elliott; *Measurement in Practice* (August/September 1997) *Issue 9*, Houston, TX: American Productivity & Quality Center (APQC) © 1997. Reprinted with permission. Contact APQC for full text.

Baldrige National Quality Program (1999). *Malcolm Baldrige National Quality Award: Profiles of Winners.* Gaithersburg, MD: National Institute of Standards and Technology.

CHAPTER 4

Create Your Scorecard

In this chapter, Vince creates his initial scorecard with help from his staff. He encounters and overcomes some initial resistance and misunderstanding about his intentions and the purpose of using scorecards. Once the line managers understand the desired outcome and expectations for their involvement, they become willing participants, and initial results exceed Vince's expectations. They conclude the meeting with plans to begin using the scorecard during regular monthly performance reviews.

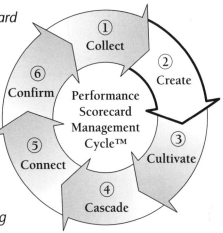

The day arrived for Vince's team to conduct its Scorecard Development Session. All of Vince's direct reports were present in the conference room when Vince and Bob came in:

⇨ Catherine Miller, Help Desk Manager;

⇨ Max McFarland, Work Station Services Manager;

⇨ Anne Bowman, Network Services Manager;

⇨ Miguel Rodriguez, Technology Integration Manager;

⇨ Holly Martin, Process Improvement Specialist; and

⇨ Libby Bates, Executive Assistant.

Create

Steps

1. Review Scorecard Development Planning Inputs
2. Define Key Result Areas
3. Relate Business Objectives to Key Result Areas
4. Brainstorm Potential Measures
5. Select the Key Indicators for Your Performance Scorecard
6. Define the Key Indicators
7. Develop Action Plans for Compiling and Reviewing the Key Indicators

Prior to the meeting, Vince had asked his team to review the information suggested by Bob. Vince opened the meeting by welcoming everyone and introducing Bob. Vince explained that they were going to develop a scorecard to address performance concerns and turned the floor over to Bob.

Bob spent a few minutes explaining the purpose of a Performance Scorecard and the process the team would use to develop Vince's scorecard. He concluded his opening remarks by saying, "So, our outcomes for the day are a clear set of team objectives, scorecard measures tied to objectives, and action plans for moving forward. Any questions?"

"Just one," Max said, "Vince, I read the preview materials and brought the things you asked, but why are we doing this? Don't we already have enough measures?"

"Of course," Vince responded, "more than enough measures. We don't want to create additional measures, but we want to identify the vital few measures that we need to improve our team's performance. Later, we'll repeat the exercise for each of you to determine how your respective measures match and align to our team measures."

"I'm not sure this is a good use of our time, but I'll tag along for now," Max said.

"Thank you, Max. I think you will find this worthwhile," Vince said. "Take it away, Bob."

Create

Step 1

Review Scorecard Development Planning Inputs

"To start, let's look at your planning inputs," Bob said. "All of you have copies of Jan Larson's goals for the current year. I'm sure all of you know the importance of increasing revenues and profits, improving customer satisfaction, expanding markets, and improving service performance."

"I understand them," Catherine said, "but I have a hard time figuring how to connect with them. I'm on the help desk. What do I have to do with revenues, profits, and expanding markets? That's all sales stuff over in Gene Ellis' shop."

"Yeah, we all know that customer satisfaction is out of our hands," Miguel said. "We do a great job with services, but Gene Ellis' sales guys make all these promises on schedules we can't keep. Customers get upset when we miss appointments, and how are we supposed to improve satisfaction that way?"

> **Expert Tip**
>
> Review corporate goals and measures to identify the priorities for your team's outputs and contributions.

Everyone began arguing at the same time over the objectives. Vince had to call the meeting to order.

"All right, settle down," Vince said. "We know there are issues with our business objectives. That's why we're here. We'll find areas where objectives and measures don't make sense. Bob, let's move on."

"Let's identify your team's key result areas, which are critical, must-achieve, make-or-break business outcomes," Bob said. "Think of them as categories of business results. These might include 'financial returns,' 'market growth,' 'customer 'satisfaction,' 'employee development,' 'service quality,' or others. Here are some guidelines for identifying key result areas."

> **Create**
>
> **Step 2**
>
> Define Key Result Areas

Bob referred to the following guidelines he had written on a flip chart.

- ➪ What primary products or services are delivered to customers?
- ➪ What business results are emphasized by management?
- ➪ What results consume the majority of team resources?
- ➪ What categories of results are defined in customer agreements?
- ➪ What categories of results are defined by corporate strategies?

After some discussion, Bob and the team identified four key result areas tied to SolvNET strategic goals, as follows:

SolvNET Strategic Goals	Vince's Key Result Areas
Build customer loyalty with each transaction	Customer Satisfaction
Grow profitably	Financial Fitness
Develop lean and efficient work systems	Workplace Excellence
Achieve a competitive advantage with employee knowledge, skills, and capabilities	Associate Proficiency

"Good," Bob said. "Our next step is to review your team's objectives and relate them to the key result areas. Objectives relate to outcomes, results, or outputs, while key result areas are really categories of outcomes. So, you may have one or more objective for each key result area."

| **Create**
Step 3
Relate Business Objectives to Key Result Areas |

"There are important characteristics of objectives. They should relate to strategic goals, align with your company's vision, and be specific, measurable, achievable, realistic, and time-based. Let's look at yours."

Bob listed the department's objectives on a flip chart:

- ⇨ Increase customer satisfaction by 10 percent by end of the year;

- ⇨ Improve service quality to customers 10 percent by end of the year;

- ⇨ Lower service quality costs by 10 percent by mid-year; and

- ⇨ Increase revenues and profits 10 percent by end of the year.

"Vince explained to me that you set your team's goals around the theme to 'Improve NET by Ten,' with a goal to improve performance by 10 percent in all areas," Bob said.

"Right, and we're having a tough time meeting some of these goals. For some targets, I can't tell whether we're making progress or not," Vince said.

"I can tell you we're making progress in the service quality with reductions in network outages," Anne Bowman said, "but the 10 percent goal across the board is way too high. We were already at industry standards last year. We won't be able to afford a 10 percent improvement without major investments in new equipment."

"Yeah, and the 10 percent reduction in work station installation time is going to require more technicians," Max said. "So, either I hire more or Anne gives up some of her people to handle the volume."

Anne and Max began arguing over resource needs and problems related to achieving targets. Vince had to call them to order again.

"All right, everyone," Vince said. "We're not here today to solve resource problems. Let's get back to measures. Bob, what happens next?"

"Let's see how your objectives match to your key result areas," Bob said as he wrote the following on the flip chart.

Team Key Result Areas	Team Objectives
Customer Satisfaction	Increase customer satisfaction by 10 percent by end of the year
Financial Fitness	Increase revenues and profits 10 percent by end of the year
Workplace Excellence	Improve service quality to customers 10 percent by end of the year
	Lower service quality costs by 10 percent by mid-year
Associate Proficiency	

Expert Tip

Characteristics of Effective Measures:
- Easily understood
- Controllable by team actions
- Reflect actual performance changes
- Align with objectives
- Reliable and true
- Traceable to a source

"Look," Holly said, "We have a key result area with no objective. Should that happen?"

"No," Bob said, "Not unless there are special reasons that exclude your team from a particular area. Since you have employees, you should have objectives for associate proficiency."

"We sure need to build product knowledge on the help desk," Catherine said.

"And our people need training on the latest network systems," Anne said.

"Frankly, we could use training on all aspects of new technology," Miguel admitted. "Plus, we need some training in problem resolution, complaint management, and other topics. I suggest we do a needs assessment first, and then prioritize the needs."

"Great idea, Miguel," Holly said. "I don't mind doing the needs analysis with everyone's cooperation." Everyone agreed to support Holly with the needs analysis.

"Good," Vince said, "let's add an objective to 'complete a needs analysis within 90 days.' Then, we'll update our associate proficiency objective based on the outcomes. Holly, does that give you enough time?"

"Sure," Holly agreed.

"OK, our next step is to brainstorm our measures," Bob said. "A measure is a concrete indicator of how well our team is doing on a given objective or outcome. A comprehensive set of measures, that is, a Performance Scorecard, provides an accurate, complete picture of performance toward objectives."

> # Create
> **Step 4**
> Brainstorm Potential Measures

"But we already have lots of measures, Vince," Max said. "What's this really all about? Do you want to see more detail of what we're doing every day?"

"I know we have lots of measures," Vince said. "Actually, I'm trying to see whether we can eliminate some and minimize the number I have to monitor. According to experts, I should be able to monitor fewer than twenty measures. And so should each of you."

The group was momentarily stunned. "Twenty?" Catherine cried. "How can I manage the help desk with only twenty measures? I now review hundreds." The other managers began talking at once about the difficulty in reducing the number of measures they used.

"Hold on, everybody. Catherine, how many measures provide useful feedback now? How many do you really watch closely and use for decision making?" Bob asked.

Catherine thought for a moment. "Maybe you're right. There are only a few that I watch closely, and that number is probably under twenty. There are some that I wonder why we track. I'm OK with going on to see whether I could eliminate some." The other managers nodded concurrence.

Bob said, "Great, the next step is to brainstorm measures for each objective." Bob explained characteristics of effective measures and how the measures would be evaluated. As Bob wrote their ideas down, Vince and his team brainstormed the following key measures for Vince's scorecard.

Objective: Increase Customer Satisfaction by 10 Percent

⇨   Customer Satisfaction Ratings

⇨   Number of Customer Feedback Cards Returned

⇨   Number of Customer Ratings Obtained

⇨   Percent of Customers Providing Feedback

⇨   Number of Customer Complaints

Objective: Increase Revenues and Profits 10 Percent

⇨ Department Revenues

⇨ Department Net Profits

⇨ Percent Budget Variance

⇨ Profit per Service Area

Objective: Improve Service Quality to Customers 10 Percent

⇨ Percent Service Requests Completed on Time

⇨ Percent Service Requests Needing Rework

⇨ Service Request Response Time

⇨ Number of Service Requests Missed

⇨ Reasons Service Requests Missed

⇨ Number of Network Outages

⇨ Length of Network Outages

⇨ Service Request Completion Time

Objective: Lower Service Quality Costs by 10 Percent

⇨ Service Center Expenses

⇨ Cost Per Help Desk Call

⇨ Cost Per Service Request

⇨ Cost Per Network Node

⇨ Cost Per Employee

Objective: Complete a Needs Analysis Within 90 Days

⇨ Number of Skill Needs Identified from Needs Analysis

⇨ Percent of Employees with Needs Analysis Completed

⇨ Number of Training Courses Completed

⇨ Number of Training Courses Needed

⇨ Percent of Employees Trained in Key Skills

The team studied the list for a moment. Max said, "Vince, how about twenty-seven measures? They all look important to me."

"They may all be important," Vince said, "but they are not all ones I need to see. Let me pick out the ones I need." He marked several off the list, ending up with the list shown in Figure 4.1 below.

"You wanted fewer than twenty measures, Vince," Miguel said. "How about seven?"

Team Objectives	Measures
Increase Customer Satisfaction by 10 Percent	Customer Satisfaction Ratings
Increase Revenues and Profits 10 Percent by End of the Year	Department Revenues Department Net Profits
Improve Service Quality to Customers 10 Percent by End of the Year	Percent Service Requests Completed on Time Percent Service Requests Needing Rework
Lower Service Quality Costs by 10 Percent by Mid-Year	Service Center Expenses
Complete a Needs Analysis Within 90 days	Number of Skill Needs Identified

Figure 4.1. *Vince's Vital Few Scorecard Measures*

Vince studied the list. "If I could see these numbers every month and know they were accurate, I would be very comfortable," he said. "Of course, I'd need to know that each of you had your portion of each measure and that you were watching your expenses, customer satisfaction, and service performance."

Create

Step 5

Select the Key Indicators for Your Performance Scorecard

"We've been telling you that for weeks," Anne said. "We want ownership and feedback for our areas of responsibility. Right now, we monitor lots more than we need to because we're not sure which indicator you might target for a question."

Several side discussions began as the team swapped instances of when Vince asked for measures that no one cared about or no one tracked.

"Whoa, everybody, I see that Anne touched a nerve," Vince said. "If I'm the one creating all this extra data, I'll be the first to change. I never realized until now that my questions

Create

Step 6

Define the Key Indicators

would create extra measures and more work. But I would like to manage to these seven if I knew that all of you were supporting performance on these priorities. Bob, it looks as if we identified my vital few measures. Don't we need to determine how to identify and link the managers' measures so that they have a vital few? Would you all like fewer measures?"

A resounding "YES" came from the team. "OK," Vince said, "I think we made a breakthrough today!"

"Wonderful. We're running short on time, so let's combine Steps 6 and 7 and take an action to define our key indicators," Bob said. "Does everyone understand that key indicators are the vital few measures?" Everyone nodded understanding and agreed to combine the steps.

Vince and his team identified actions for developing their scorecard. Libby summarized them on the flip chart, as shown in Figure 4.2.

Action	Owner	Due Dates
Draft definitions and baselines for the initial set of scorecard measures	Holly and Libby	Before the end of the month
Review effectiveness of scorecard measures and check scorecard results	Entire management team	During normal weekly staff meetings
Present the key result areas, objectives, and scorecard measures to employees	Vince	At next month's "all-hands" meeting
Evaluate progress to see whether measurement definitions need to be "tweaked"	Vince and staff	Once per month for the next quarter
Review targets for each measure	Vince and staff	At the start of next quarter

Figure 4.2. *Actions for Developing SolvNET's Customer Services Scorecard*

"This has been quite a session," Bob said. "Let's wrap up with an evaluation and see what you thought of the meeting."

"I see you have evaluation forms," Catherine said. "I just want to say that I found this very worthwhile, and I see it as a positive step."

Even Max gave an affirmative murmur as Libby passed around the evaluation forms shown in Figure 4.3.

Scorecard Development Session Evaluation

Leader: _____ Meeting Date: _____

Please rate the degree to which you agree with each statement (mark appropriate response):

		Very Low Degree		Moderate Degree		Very High Degree
1.	Participants had a chance to openly express opinions and ideas.	1	2	3	4	5
2.	Participants listened to each other.	1	2	3	4	5
3.	Participants seemed satisfied with the group's decisions.	1	2	3	4	5
4.	Participants stayed focused on agenda items.	1	2	3	4	5
5.	The leader was prepared.	1	2	3	4	5
6.	Participants were prepared.	1	2	3	4	5
7.	Participants were clear about action item responsibilities.	1	2	3	4	5
8.	Participants were allowed to be creative and think "outside the box."	1	2	3	4	5

Comments/Suggestions:

Figure 4.3. *Evaluation Form*

"Just leave your completed evaluations with me," Libby said, "I'll distribute meeting minutes and action items tomorrow. Thank you."

"Thank you, Libby, for taking care of that. And thank all of you for your contributions today," Vince added. "I agree with Catherine that this is a positive first step. We'll get our baselines together and start reviewing these in our weekly staff meetings as we move to the Cultivate Phase. See you next week at our staff meeting."

After everyone left, Vince said to Bob, "Hey, that went pretty well. I think they like the idea."

"I thought they would," Bob responded with a smile.

Summary

During the Create Phase, you develop a Performance Scorecard that:

- ➪ Supports management commitments and plans;
- ➪ Monitors work processes;
- ➪ Relates to customer needs;
- ➪ Measures achievement of key business goals; and
- ➪ Clarifies responsibility and ownership.

Developing the initial Performance Scorecard measures is done by following the steps outlined in the summary table below. Once the vital few measures are selected, it is important to define the scorecard measures to clarify what is measured and how measures will be drawn from the organization. Action plans to compile the measurement data complete the Create Phase, leading to the Cultivate Phase, in which you begin reviewing the measurement results matched to your desired business outcomes.

PHASE	STEPS	OUTCOMES

Phase 2: CREATE

1. Review scorecard development planning inputs.

2. Define key result areas.

3. Relate business objectives to key result areas.

4. Brainstorm potential measures.

5. Select the key indicators for your Performance Scorecard.

6. Define the key indicators.

7. Develop action plans for compiling and reviewing the key indicators.

- Team objectives
- Scorecard measures linked to corporate goals, business objectives, and customer requirements
- Action plans to develop measures

Measurement Case Study: United Parcel Service

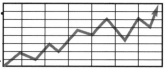

A familiar presence that delivers more than 12 million packages every day, the United Parcel Service (UPS) reestablished its emphasis on quality and performance in 1996. Four elements formed the foundation of the corporate emphasis: *leadership, people, processes,* and *measurement.*

Leadership built its foundation with managers whose responsibility it was to:

➪ Guide implementation of quality efforts and efficiency;

➪ Track, measure, and evaluate the effectiveness of the operating plan;

➪ Evaluate, migrate, and integrate business and quality initiatives; and

➪ Help managers, employees, and groups establish priorities focusing on improvement efforts and results.

Systematic, organized methods were developed for improving four strategic UPS processes covering:

➪ Developing and maintaining internal and external customers;

➪ Picking up, transporting, and delivering ground parcels;

➪ Billing and collecting revenue;

➪ Developing and introducing new products and services;

➪ Responding to internal and external customer inquiries; and

➪ Providing data and information to internal and external customers.

Measurement improvements included UPS's Quality Improvement Process (QIP) that aligned the company's measurement system with its quality improvement goals. Using a scorecard approach, UPS's QIP divides critical business information into four main areas:

➪ Customers (how UPS customers see UPS);

➪ People, innovation, and learning (how UPS is perceived by UPS employees);

➪ Financial (UPS's economic well-being); and

➪ Internal business processes (the details of how UPS conducts its business).

54

Mike Brown, UPS corporate quality manager during QIP development, said, "There are two important concepts involved here. One is a broadening of the focus to include items other than traditional financial and performance measures. A second is the importance of balancing the areas to be measured. No single measure can provide a clear view of the business. It takes a balanced view of each important area to be successful in today's business environment."

To date, the result is a 15 percent increase in operational performance. "This increase in productivity is not because people are doing anything different or because they are working harder," Brown said. "UPS looked at its processes, leveraged technology in the operations, and eliminated steps that added no value. The ability to track packages meticulously along every step of their journey has given UPS outstanding control of its processes."

"UPS: Its Long-Term Design Delivers Quality Millions of Times Each Day" by Brad Stratton. *Quality Progress* (October 1998). Milwaukee, WI: American Society for Quality. Copyright © 1998 American Society for Quality. Reprinted with Permission.

CHAPTER 5

Cultivate Your Scorecard

In this chapter, Vince learns how to use his scorecard to monitor performance, interpret performance levels, and determine appropriate actions to take. He is able to identify gaps in the measurement information that is available to manage performance, and he assigns people to take action to close the gaps.

Vince also learns how to set appropriate targets, measure improvement, and strengthen links between scorecards. He begins to realize the benefits of managing with scorecards by more quickly identifying problems, aligning work processes, and linking employee efforts with business targets.

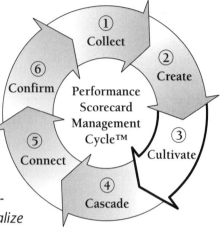

Vince's anticipation grew as the day approached for his team to review the new scorecard. Holly was busy assembling charts and refused to give Vince a preview. She said she wanted to surprise him with her thoroughness and the way the information was laid out.

Review day arrived and Vince's team assembled in the conference room. Bob was

Cultivate

Steps

1. Gather, Display, and Analyze Historical Data
2. Conduct Performance Reviews
3. Determine Appropriate Targets
4. Develop Improvement Action Plans
5. Strengthen Horizontal and Vertical Linkages

unable to attend due to a prior commitment, but the same team that created the scorecard was present: Catherine, Max, Anne, Miguel, Holly, and Libby.

Several discussions were underway as Vince entered. "All right, everyone, let's get started," Vince said. "Our main agenda item is to review our scorecard. Holly, are you ready?"

Cultivate

Step 1

Gather, Display, and Analyze
Historical Data

"I sure am," Holly enthused.

Libby dimmed the lights as Holly switched on the electronic projector and displayed her first chart. "Recall that we identified seven key measures for our scorecard," Holly began. "I gathered the data from a variety of sources, and here are our first results. Let's start with customer satisfaction."

Holly's Customer Satisfaction Chart is shown in Figure 5.1.

"Customer satisfaction ratings are coming down from last year and . . .," Holly began.

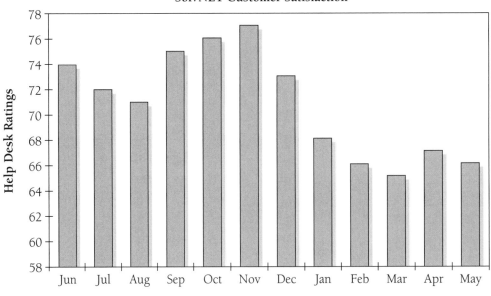

Figure 5.1. *SolvNET Customer Satisfaction Ratings*

"Wait a minute, Holly," Anne said. "Ratings seem to be going down because we changed the rating scale. Scores are actually better than last year's, but you haven't adjusted scores for the new scale."

"Why is this only the customer ratings from the help desk?" Catherine asked. "What about the feedback cards and the ratings we get from quarterly customer interviews?"

"Why are the ratings shown on a hundred-point scale?" Max queried. "I thought help desk ratings were on a scale of 1 to 5."

Holly looked dumbfounded as Libby muttered, "Oh dear, I should have seen this coming."

"Seen what?" Vince asked. "That we would argue over customer satisfaction results?"

"Actually, yes," Libby said, "not just customer satisfaction results, but all our results. This isn't Holly's fault. We needed to complete our action to clarify and define each of the measures before we sent Holly out to gather data."

"You mean we've wasted two weeks gathering data and now we won't see the results?" Vince asked testily. He was thinking about another call from Jan Larson that morning asking about his team's progress with results.

"No, the time wasn't wasted, but we have more to do," Libby explained. "Our first review has to include a discussion of what is measured and how measures are defined."

> ## Cultivate
> **Step 2**
> Conduct Performance Reviews

"Libby, what do you suggest we do?" Vince asked as he regained his composure.

"We need to agree on the definition for our customer satisfaction measure," Libby said. "Then, let's look at the results that Holly pulled together for the other measures. We need to see what she found and agree whether it's the right data. Our first step is to understand what is measured."

Vince paused. "Thanks, Libby, that's just what we'll do. All right, team, what's the right measure for customer service?"

"Since we have three indicators for customer satisfaction, I say we average all three together," Max said.

"How can we?" Catherine asked. "The help desk ratings are a percentage of customers who rated us four or better on our five-point rating scale. The feedback cards are an average from a five-point rating, and the interview results are reported on a one through ten rating scale."

The team looked at each other for a way to combine the measures. "Sounds like a good question for Bob when he returns," Vince said. "Libby, will you note the action to discuss ways to combine the customer satisfaction measures with Bob?" Libby nodded and jotted a note.

"Holly, what's next?" Vince asked. Holly showed her next chart, for department expenses, shown in Figure 5.2.

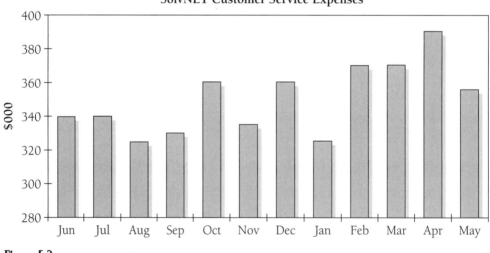

Figure 5.2. *Expenses for Vince's Department*

"Hey, look at that big drop in May—way to go, team," Catherine said.

"Sorry, didn't notice. I was too busy looking at the big spike in April," Max said.

"It looks like things are getting worse, Vince, but how do these numbers compare to our targets? Are we on track?" asked Anne.

"I was concerned that things were getting worse, and this confirms it," Vince said. "All of these are valid comments—we need to understand what's causing these numbers to jump around each month."

"I can answer that," Libby said. Everyone turned to look at her.

"Now, Libby, you're good, but how can you know what's causing our expenses to jump? You've only been here a total of two months," Vince said.

"It's called variation," Libby said.

"She's right," Holly said. "The reason May went down is because it didn't go up."

Everyone laughed. "Thank you, Holly, for that valuable insight," Vince chuckled. "Could you tell us a little more about how variation affects our expenses?"

"Sure," Holly said, "just think back to your statistics class in college."

> ⤷ **Expert Tips**
>
> - Common cause variation is the normal variation caused by ever-present factors that contribute to random shifts in outcomes.
> - Special cause variation creates an occasional jump in results and makes processes unpredictable.
> - Structural variation is a repeating pattern of trends, cycles, or seasonal changes.

Everyone groaned. "Do we have to?" pleaded Anne.

"Seriously," Holly said, "It's important to make the right decisions when you review the numbers. Start with calculating the average for expenses over the last twelve months."

"Three hundred fifty thousand dollars a month," Miguel said. Everyone turned to Miguel. "Hey, I was curious, so I calculated while you were talking."

"OK, start there," Holly continued. "Notice no month actually hit $350,000; that's just your average. Each month is a little more or a little less. Now, remember standard deviation from statistics?"

"Something about the distance from the average," Miguel said.

"Right," Holly said, "for a set of data, it's the sum of the differences squared divided by the number of observations. We can calculate the exact number, but what's more important is the idea at this point. Let's say the standard deviation is $20,000."

Holly continued, "Standard deviation relates to variation because we expect our numbers each month to vary around the average. The standard deviation tells us how much variation to expect. Based on statistical formulas, multiply the standard deviation times three and add and subtract it from the average. You get a range of numbers that determine what's expected."

"I think I'm with you," Catherine said. "Can you give us an example?"

"Sure, start with multiplying three times $20,000, or $60,000. Add $60,000 to the average of $350,000 to give you $410,000. This is called the *upper control limit.*"

> ### ☞ Expert Tip
>
> Control limits are statistically derived and define the expected range of data points based on past performance. Calculating control limits is fairly straight-forward, but depend on the type of variable you are plotting. Consult any source on Statistical Process Control if you need help calculating the control limits for your specific measures.

"I follow the math so far, but I still don't get where you're going," Max said.

"We're almost there," Holly said. "For the lower limit, subtract $60,000 from $350,000 to get $290,000. These two numbers are your *expected range.* For any month, you expect expenses around $350,000, but you shouldn't be surprised if expenses fall any-where between $290,000 and $410,000."

"But all the numbers fall in those ranges," Max said. "What does that tell us?"

"It tells us that things are pretty normal," Holly said. "We shouldn't be too alarmed about the jump in April or too excited about the drop in January. They are just normal variation in our expenses. You would probably have a hard time finding out why they jump around. If expenses go above $410,000 or below $290,000 we should look more closely. That would be an indication that something is different."

"You're right, Holly. It is helpful to understand variation and know when things are going haywire. But I'm concerned about the overall trend. Do you agree that the expense problem is getting worse? Look at them going up since January!" Vince said.

"Yes, it appears that expenses are increasing because four of our last six results are moving up," Holly said, "but random chance may be the real reason we've had four months more expensive than normal. Variation exists in all processes, so we should expect values to vary from month to month. In fact, if we don't have variation, we should re-evaluate the measure."

"OK, but I want this checked out," Vince said. "If there's a reason our expenses are climbing, we need to know."

"Agreed," Holly said, "I'll check it out and get back to everyone at our next review."

"There's more to this scorecard and measurement stuff than I first realized," said Vince. "This is interesting—let's keep going."

Holly next showed her chart for percent of service requests on time, as shown in Figure 5.3.

"Whoa, look at that," Catherine said. "We're not even close to target."

"That's because you're not capable," Libby said.

"Excuse me?" Max said.

> # Cultivate
> **Step 3**
> Determine Appropriate Targets

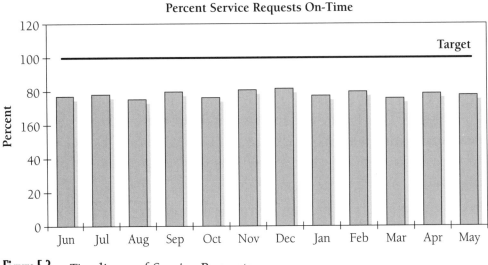

Figure 5.3. *Timeliness of Service Requests*

"Oops, I meant to say that your process is not capable. You can't hit the target because you have never hit the target," Libby said.

"She's right," Holly said. "Process capability relates to targets. If we hit a target consistently, we simply have to operate our current process at the same costs and resource levels."

"Right, but I don't want to set a target that you can hit now. What's the point of a target?" Vince said.

Holly said, "If we set a target that the process can't currently achieve, we have to change the process capability. In this case, our process can't hit the target of 99 percent until we change the process."

"Can't we hit the target by motivating our team to work harder?" Vince said.

"But our guys are already stretched to the limit," Max said. "I've been concerned that we'll never hit this target. We just need more people."

"More people won't help you if the process won't support the target. You need to look at all the factors in the process to determine whether workload, cycle time, and other factors will allow you to ever hit 99 percent—or, even better, 100 percent on time," Holly said.

"I'm starting to see why we need a scorecard," Miguel said. "There's a lot to our business that we don't understand!"

The team continued its review, uncovering false assumptions, misinformation, and gaps in knowledge about performance. This is typical of teams just beginning to develop Performance Scorecards, which illustrates the need to *cultivate* the scorecard, develop-

> ## Cultivate
>
> **Step 4**
>
> Develop Improvement Action Plans

ing a true picture of performance with the vital few. The group took several actions for obtaining more information, clarifying definitions, and refining the charts.

"Well, it looks as if we have our work cut out for us," Catherine said. "We need to figure out some of our targets and even some of our measures."

"Hey, no wonder we were struggling in some areas! We didn't even know what to measure," Anne noted.

Vince nodded, "This scorecard stuff really brings it home. That should just about do us for today. Let's plan to meet two weeks from today to look at this again. Thank you, Holly, for preparing our charts. I realize we won't have next month's results, but I want to continue refining the charts. Thank you all. This has certainly been an eye-opener."

As Vince and Libby headed back toward Vince's office, Libby noted Vince's silence. "Thinking about today's review?" she asked.

"It was a real learning experience," Vince admitted. "I never realized we had all this confusion about our performance."

"That's why we're doing a scorecard," Libby said. "I remember Bob helping us through this phase at my former company. Why don't you call him?"

Vince nodded, "I will."

Vince called Bob as soon as he entered the office. "Bob, that was a lesson in humility today."

Bob laughed, "Never realized you knew so little, eh?"

Vince summarized the outcomes and the lessons from the meeting: "So, we're going to review targets and definitions at our next meeting."

"Vince, your team made several discoveries today that are typical the first time a group reviews a scorecard," Bob said. "How about I join you at the next review and we summarize a few lessons learned and refine the measures some more before the Cascade Step?"

"I was hoping you would suggest that," Vince laughed.

Two weeks later, the team met to follow up from their last review. Vince welcomed everyone back and explained the meeting purpose: to re-examine the most recent performance results, check actions from the previous review, and continue refining the scorecard.

"Before we get into today's review," Vince said, "I asked Bob to help us summarize a few lessons learned from last time."

"Thanks, Vince," Bob said. "It sounds as though your team realized the usual experience from an initial scorecard review. There was confusion over definitions, targets, measures, and trends. That's good."

"How can that be so good?" Max said.

"Because you're bringing measurement and performance issues to the surface," Bob said. "You've been trying to manage with an incomplete and unclear picture with your old measures. As you *cultivate,* you clear up the confusion and develop a scorecard that everyone understands and aligns to your business."

"So, you're on the right track," Bob continued. "To help with today's review, I'll list a few items to check as you go through today's results. I call them 'Measure Mints.'" Bob said.

"Hey, I like that," Catherine said.

"You would," Max muttered.

Bob turned the page on the flip chart and wrote the following:

"Measure Mint" 1:
Prepare Complete Performance Summaries

"As you develop charts, make it easy for participants to understand and interpret the charts," Bob explained. "Be sure to include the following items." Bob added to the flip chart:

⇨ Title of the measure;

⇨ At least twelve periods (days, weeks, or months) of historical data, if available;

⇨ Target level(s);

⇨ Control limits;

⇨ Benchmarks and/or best competitor's targets; and

⇨ Projected targets.

"When possible, use colors to distinguish key features such as target lines, control lines, trend lines, and benchmarks."

"Good, we'll check each chart as we go through them," Holly said.

Bob turned over the next flip-chart page and wrote the following:

"Measure Mint" 2: Preview Performance Summaries

"Before assembling the review team, preview the charts. Note any unusual spikes or drops and list questions for the review about items like these." Bob wrote on the flip chart:

⇨ Undesired trends;

⇨ Values beyond control limits;

⇨ Values that don't match the other sources of feedback;

- ⇨ Measures you don't understand; and
- ⇨ Measures not meeting standards of customer requirements or performance targets.

"Contact people, as appropriate, to provide a 'heads-up' that questions will be discussed at the review," Bob said. "Don't try to address all the questions before the review, but provide an opportunity for individuals to prepare a response."

"Good point. We didn't do this," Vince said. "Holly, let's be sure to preview the charts before the next review." Holly nodded her agreement.

Bob moved to the next easel page and wrote:

"Measure Mint" 3: Assemble the Appropriate Team

"The most important factor in using your scorecard to support ongoing improvement is to provide feedback to the right team," Bob said. "Vince, I'm glad that you've assembled your managers for these reviews. It's the right thing to do."

"Should I have anyone else here?" Vince asked. "Like my boss or the other VPs?"

"Probably not," Bob said. "The proper team is determined by the measurements. The next-level manager should be included when issues surface that affect the next level up. As a general rule, you shouldn't invite your boss unless issues affect her. But you should attend her scorecard review. And you should brief her as soon as your scorecard comes together. She needs to be aware of your measures and ensure alignment with her priorities."

Bob continued, "When deciding on the audience for the review, keep the following rule of thumb in mind." He wrote on the flip chart:

- ⇨ Involve the people who affect and are affected by changes in the results.

"Makes good sense," Miguel said. "What's next?"

Bob flipped to the next easel page and wrote:

"Measure Mint" 4: Review Results—With a Purpose

"During the review, you want your audience to do four things," Bob said. He added this list on the flip chart:

⇨ Understand what is measured;

⇨ Compare performance to a standard (that is, a target, prior performance, a customer expectation, or an industry benchmark);

⇨ Identify and discuss significant exceptions to normal performance; and

⇨ Define actions to reinforce good performance or investigate bad performance.

"That's a nice summary of what I had in mind as I prepared the charts," Holly said.

"Good," Bob said as he flipped to the next page:

"Measure Mint" 5: Challenge the Values

"All right, now we're getting into something that sounds like fun," Max said.

"You want to manage by fact, but use your intuition and common sense," Bob said. "If you know that performance in an area was poor, but the values show an increase, challenge the value. Consider the following questions when the value seems wrong."

⇨ Was the right data included in the calculation?

⇨ Was the value calculated correctly?

⇨ Did the data cover the performance period shown on the graph?

⇨ Is the value calculated and reported consistently from one period to the next?

⇨ Did we have the right values last period?

"So, question the numbers each time they're shown?" Anne said.

"Just be aware that results can change sometimes by the way values are calculated and reported without a true underlying change in performance. It's something you want to watch, especially early in the Cultivate Phase," Bob said. He flipped to the next page and wrote:

"Measure Mint" 6:
Discuss Trends and Performance Anomalies

Bob said, "Definitions of 'trend' vary, and the true statistical definition is rigorous for workplace measurements. Two data points in a row in a consecutive direction, up or down, are not considered a trend. Here's a useful rule of thumb." He wrote on the flip chart:

⇨ A "trend" consists of six consecutive points that fall above (or below) the average value.

⇨ Three points in a row above (or below) the average do not define a trend, but give a warning to examine the system.

"In the reality of the workplace, managers rarely have the opportunity to report six consecutive periods of declining performance before actions are demanded," Bob said.

"That's for sure," Anne noted with a glance toward Vince.

"Although you often can't wait for the next data point to see whether there is a trend, you should not panic when you see two or even three consecutive declines, unless there are dramatic drops," Bob said. "Don't act prematurely without some evidence of a trend, so use the rule of thumb and common sense. But for big changes that can't be explained, be sure to investigate."

"Oh, our boss would never panic or jump to an investigation too early," Catherine said. Everyone broke into laughter, including Vince.

"Similarly, if you are trying to improve results, but the measurement is not moving, challenge the measure with the following." Bob wrote on the flip chart:

⇨ Does the improvement initiative need more time to mature?

⇨ Is the initiative well-defined and deployed?

⇨ Are improvement efforts linked to the right measures?

"Next item," Bob said as he flipped the page and wrote:

"Measure Mint" 7: Assign Appropriate Actions

Bob wrote this list beneath the item:

⇨   Actions must be specific and actionable;

⇨   Actions must be deployed;

⇨   Actions must be linked to a measurement; and

⇨   Actions must be followed up.

"If you suggest that 'someone needs to see whether this result is getting out of hand,' every member of the review team will interpret 'getting out of hand' differently," Bob explained. "Instead, ask a specific team member to compare the latest result to the average from the last four quarters and report back at the next review."

"Consider who should be involved in the action," Bob continued. "Who needs to inform the people affected? What are they expected to do to change performance? Do they need a briefing, training, or an incentive? Make sure the right people know they have an action to take.

"Next, test your assumptions about actions and measures by predicting which measures will change as a result of the action. How much will the measurement change? How soon should a change be noticed?

"Finally, take notes during the review and distribute them after the meeting, highlighting any assigned actions. At the next session, review the follow-up actions for closure," Bob concluded.

"That's all good advice," Vince said. "Bob, can you tape those around the room for us to consider while we do our review? Libby, when we're done, will you type them up so we'll have a record?"

"Of course," Libby said as Bob began taping the sheets to the walls.

"I'm sure we're all ready to begin," Vince said. "Holly, our first chart, please."

Holly began with the chart on customer satisfaction. They brought up the previous issue of how to combine multiple measures. They explained the three different measures they now used. Bob acknowledged that he would take the data and show them how to combine the measures at the next meeting.

The team continued through the charts, listing areas for improvement based on Bob's suggestions. Holly showed results for the percent of service repairs needing rework shown in Figure 5.4.

"So, our percent of service repairs needing rework dropped last month to less than 5 percent, our best score in six months," Holly said.

"But what's our target?" Catherine asked. "If the target is 5 percent, we're doing great, but if it's 1 percent, we're still way off."

"The target is zero," Vince said. "We don't want any rework."

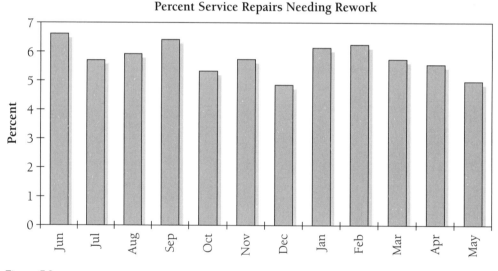

Figure 5.4. *Rework Percentage for Repairs*

Performance Scorecards

"You can set a target of zero if you want, but we still don't have the capability to hit it," Max said. "Remember our discussion last time about capability? Arbitrary targets do more harm than good."

"Max is right," Bob said. "Target setting is probably the hardest thing about using measures and scorecards. You have to think carefully because there are four sources of information to use when determining targets."

Bob listed four sources of targets on the flip chart:

⇨   Statistics related to past performance and process capability;

⇨   Customer requirements;

⇨   Industry benchmarks and competitive assessments; and

⇨   Corporate expectations.

"Let's look at each source and determine how we select the right one," Bob said. "The first way is to chart past performance. From your historical data, you can set appropriate targets. There are four types of targets you can set based on past performance." He listed the following:

1.   Every result must be above the historical average;

2.   Every result must be below the historical average;

3.   The average result must be above the historical average; or

4.   The average result must be below the historical average.

"We're just considering the average here for your rework results. There may be other statistical results to consider, such as upper or lower control limits. But we'll keep it simple for this illustration," Bob said.

"For our percent of service repairs needing rework, we might consider a Type 2 target," Bob continued. "On the other hand, if we want this year's average results to be better than last year's average, we set a Type 4 target. We can set statistical targets if we don't have a lot of information about customer or market requirements. Also, statistical targets are often used for detailed, process-level measures."

"What if customers don't care what your statistics say—they just want less rework. In fact, they will expect zero rework! How do you set your target?" Vince asked.

"In many cases, targets are defined by customers," Bob explained. "That's the second source of targets. If so, clarify the target with your customer: Is this the minimum expected level? An average performance level? The desired high-performance target? We have to match the customer's target against our historical performance to determine whether we are capable of achieving and sustaining targeted levels."

"It makes sense to respond to customer targets, but what if customers don't know, or what if we want to gain an advantage over our competitors?" Anne asked.

"An excellent point, and the third way to determine a target," Bob said. "Industry-driven targets are needed sometimes to catch or pass our competitors."

"These are all fine, but I'll tell you where we get most of our targets," Vince said. Everyone turned to him. "My boss. Jan Larson has a lot of targets handed to her from corporate, especially financial targets."

"Thanks, Vince, for bringing up the fourth source of targets," Bob said. "Regardless of the source, we have to determine the gap between past performance and the new level of expected performance."

"All the more reason for a good scorecard!" Miguel said. "So, Vince, what are the targets for our scorecard measures?"

Vince went to the whiteboard and listed the key measures for customer services, as shown in Figure 5.5.

Vince said, "We have our financial goals. Holly, can you calculate our averages and suggest targets for the customer and service measures based on statistical

Objectives	Measure	Targets
Increase customer satisfaction by 10 percent	Customer Satisfaction Ratings	TBD: Need to define measure
Increase revenues and profits 10 percent by end of the year	Department Revenues Department Net Profits	$5.0M $1.0M
Improve service quality to customers 10 percent by the end of the year	Percent Service Requests Completed on Time Percent Service Requests Needing Rework	TBD TBD
Lower service quality costs by 10 percent by mid-year	Service Center Expenses	$4.0M

Figure 5.5. *SolvNET's Customer Services Targets*

history? I'd like for all of us to know what to expect based on past performance." Holly nodded.

"That's great," Bob said. "You're right where you should be and are doing the right things to cultivate your scorecard. Just one last thing—don't forget to check your vertical and horizontal links."

"Yes, I saw that as the next step," Vince said. "Exactly how do we do that, Bob?"

Bob explained, "To reinforce vertical linkages, share your objectives and measures with teams up and down your organization. Check for links and consistencies between your goals and measures and your boss's goals and measures.

You want aligned measures, but that doesn't mean the same measures at each level. Make sure that your boss isn't tracking detailed measures and that front-line work teams aren't trying to operate with strategic-level summary measures."

<table>
<tr><td>

Cultivate

Step 5

Strengthen Horizontal and
Vertical Linkages
</td></tr>
</table>

"Categorize your scorecard measures according to your key result areas," Bob continued. "Consider whether you have measures for each key result area."

"Right," Catherine agreed. "We already saw one key result area with no measure and took steps to fix that."

"Good!" Bob said, "You're really growing with this. Also, check whether the measures match the responsibilities assigned by your boss and your position. If you identify some measures that don't fit the key result areas, check whether you should eliminate the measure, re-examine the key result area, or review the responsibility with your boss."

"OK, I see the steps for checking vertical linkages. What about horizontal linkages?" Vince asked.

"Your scorecard should provide an end-to-end look at processes driving your business results," Bob explained. "You want a broad view of what's coming into your team, how your team is performing, and what is flowing out of your team. You need a line of sight to the entire work process to ensure that customers' requirements are fulfilled."

"Like our measure for tracking service orders completed on time and percent reworked? Will those give us the right end-to-end view?" Vince asked.

"That's a good start," Bob said. "You'll identify some better ones as you and your managers develop more sophisticated measures within your work processes."

"To strengthen horizontal linkages, discuss your team's objectives, targets, and measures with your primary customers and suppliers," Bob continued. "Ask them for their objectives, then look for mismatches between your targets and their objectives. They'll be glad you took the initiative, and your team's job will be easier because you're in greater alignment with customers' expectations."

"This is tremendous," Vince said. "We appreciate your help." The team responded favorably and agreed to meet in two weeks for their next review with fresh data from a new month.

After they concluded the meeting, Vince sat quietly and thought for a moment alone in his office. After a few minutes, a smile came over his face. He picked up the phone and made an appointment with his boss, Jan Larson. He wanted to show her his scorecard and start alignment discussions the next day.

Summary

During the Cultivate Phase, you use and improve your Performance Scorecard by completing the following steps, which are summarized in the chart below:

⇨   Displaying and analyzing historical data;

⇨   Conducting performance reviews with the people affected by the results;

⇨   Determining targets based on requirements and system capabilities; and

⇨   Executing improvement actions based on results.

Linkages to other scorecards become more apparent during this phase, providing improved line of sight up, down, and across your business. As you refine your scorecard measures and settle into the vital few measures, you set the stage for the Cascade Phase, during which you will define front-line scorecard measures and reinforce links between strategic goals and front-line process measures for your work teams.

PHASE	STEPS	OUTCOMES

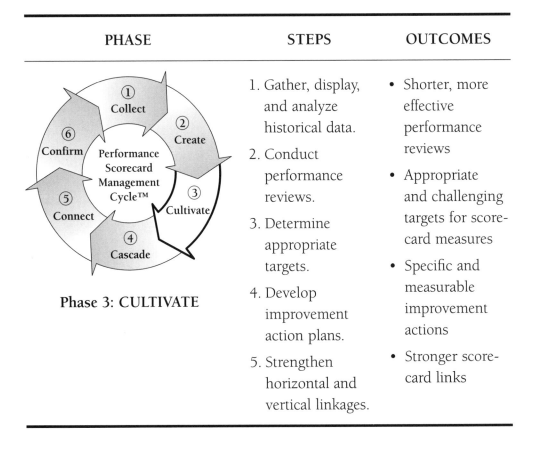

Phase 3: CULTIVATE

1. Gather, display, and analyze historical data.

2. Conduct performance reviews.

3. Determine appropriate targets.

4. Develop improvement action plans.

5. Strengthen horizontal and vertical linkages.

- Shorter, more effective performance reviews

- Appropriate and challenging targets for score-card measures

- Specific and measurable improvement actions

- Stronger score-card links

Measurement Case Study: Bekaert UBISA

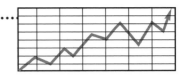

An APQC Measurement Case Study

Performance measurement at Bekaert UBISA is not an overnight success story, but one of evolution—an evolution of ideas and practices that helped the company lower costs, involve employees, and achieve positive results. Sparked by a period of poor performance 16 years ago, this manufacturer of tire cord and bead wire for tire reinforcement, based in Burgos, Spain, has continuously sought better methods to gauge progress and effect favorable change.

The overall goal has been to advance Bekaert UBISA, a 368-employee company that generated more than $60 million in sales last year as part of the Belgium-based Bekaert Group, which has 68 factories and more than 17,000 employees in 23 countries. This was done by linking UBISA's mission to the corporate mission with progress indicators.

Twelve mini-companies within UBISA—decentralized units representing the major manufacturing, support, and administrative functions—advance strategy and drive continuous quality improvement using measures. Performance indicators are always linked to the Bekaert's core dimensions: quality, cost, delivery, safety, and morale.

The core dimensions of the UBISA performance measurement system are grouped into three categories: customers, cost, and people. To track performance in the three categories, each mini-company developed a scorecard that spelled out goals and progress indicators for the categories. Once targets for each progress indicator were identified, action plans were developed to ensure that those targets were reached.

For example, the *customers* category contained three goals:

➪   Reduce customer claims;

➪   Improve deliveries on time; and

➪   Enhance cooperation with customers.

For each goal, corresponding measures were established. Progress for reducing customer claims was tracked with the indicator of "number of rejects." For deliveries on time, the progress indicator was "percent delayed lots," and cooperation with customers was monitored with "number of joint projects."

Similar goals and progress indicators were seen within the cost and people categories. With the *cost* category, goals were defined for cash cost, internal defect cost, process fractures, and machine efficiency. Corresponding progress indicators included:

⇨ Percent reduction for cash cost—a comparison of actual cash cost (monthly and year-to-date) with that of the previous year;

⇨ Cost/ton for internal defect cost—an indicator for the cost of scrap and rework hours;

⇨ Breaks/ton for process fractures; and

⇨ Percent output versus standard—an indicator of machine efficiency to a comparison to an assigned standard.

Within the *people* dimension, goals and their respective progress indicators (in parentheses) included:

⇨ Accidents (number of accidents);

⇨ Absenteeism (percent of absenteeism);

⇨ Improvement in the plant (number of improvement exercises following the methodology of benchmarking, failure mode and effect analysis, and "seven tools"); and

⇨ Development of competencies management (number of advanced competency levels in three positions—process engineer, supervisor, and foreman).

All eleven goals for the measurement scorecard were evaluated and reviewed systematically. All goals had a range of five degrees of performance: optimum, high, normal, low, and nonacceptable.

According to UBISA, the elements that contributed most to the successful implementation of performance measurement systems at the company included:

⇨ Starting with a clear mission and vision;

⇨ Basing decisions on facts and figures;

⇨ Updating the measures to match decision cycles and ensuring data were timely and accurate;

⇨ Balancing results indicators with check-point indicators to allow quicker reactions;

⇨ Linking individual performance plans to mini-company results;

⇨ Having the discipline to follow the methodology throughout implementation;

⇨ Communicating all measures, problems, and follow-ups with visual story boards and displays;

⇨ Training all employees in new skills for using measures correctly; and

⇨ Having a sense of urgency, fast follow-up, and quick reaction to deviation from parameters.

As a result, UBISA has realized control of its processes and of the creation of knowledge in the organization. This has resulted in faster decision making and quicker reactions to problems. Also, people have a better perspective on operations because of the integration of production data and cost data.

"Innovative Measurement Systems a Way of Life at Bekaert UBISA," by Craig Henderson; *Measurement in Practice, Issue 12*, Houston, TX: American Productivity & Quality Center (APQC) © 1998. Reprinted with permission. Contact APQC for full text.

CHAPTER 6

Cascade Your Scorecard

In this chapter, Vince learns how to cascade Performance Scorecard measures to his managers. As Vince applies the cascade process, he helps each manager understand how he or she contributes to the overall success of the team and how progress and contribution are monitored with scorecards. Vince begins to understand how managers' contributions "roll up" to his scorecard indicators.

Vince realizes the importance of the vital few measures and overcomes the urge to replicate identical scorecards for each manager. Vince begins to see increased accountability for results among his managers and notes improved results in selected areas.

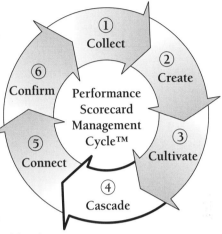

After two months of scorecard reviews, Vince's team has worked through several issues related to measurement definitions and variation. They now feel they have good visibility and understanding of the measures at Vince's level and are ready to take the next step to *cascade* Vince's scorecard to their measures.

Vince and his team are meeting to discuss the measures on each manager's scorecard. Bob provided a worksheet for the managers

Cascade

Steps

1. Determine Scorecard Measures for Next Level in the Cascade
2. Verify Cascaded Measures Are at the Appropriate Levels
3. Establish and Affirm Linkages and Alignment
4. Clarify Targets
5. Establish Summary Measures, As Needed
6. Refine Steps for Gathering, Reporting, and Reviewing Results

to identify their respective measures and is at the meeting in order to guide the team through this next phase.

"During the Cascade Phase, we see how measures from each manager's scorecard contribute to the overall success of the team," Bob explained. "Again, we want to keep our scorecards to the vital few with the right measures for accountability and feedback. To complete the worksheet, each manager reviewed his or her business objectives and determined the appropriate measures, just as we did in our initial 'create' session," Bob continued. "Each of you provided your scorecard drafts to Libby before this session. Libby compiled the drafts and brought them for review." Everyone nodded.

"Great," Bob said, "let's look at the drafts." Libby passed around the packet of drafts. The draft from Catherine Miller, help desk manager, is shown in Figure 6.1.

"Catherine, if you don't mind, we'll discuss your draft first," Bob said.

Cascade
Step 1
Determine Scorecard Measures for Next Level in the Cascade

"I don't mind being the guinea pig," Catherine replied. She explained her measures and her rationale for each.

"Shouldn't you have measures for the revenues and profits, since you have objectives?" Miguel asked.

"I think so, but I couldn't figure out what the measures are," Catherine said. "I don't have help desk revenues or profits. How is this usually handled, Bob?"

"For financial measures that can't be sliced any further, we usually put the department-level measures on the individual managers' scorecards. Sometimes it's difficult to determine how much contribution comes from each manager, but we know that all managers contribute. That way, all the managers have visibility—and accountability—toward a team target. Libby, how did they manage this at your former firm?"

"Just the way you said, Bob," Libby responded. "I remember my boss struggling with this and deciding that certain measures couldn't be sliced any further, such as revenues, profits, and customer satisfaction, in some cases."

Team Objectives	Team Measures	Catherine's Objectives	Catherine's Measures
• Increase customer satisfaction by 10 percent	• Customer Satisfaction Ratings	• Increase customer satisfaction by 10 percent	• Customers' Help Desk Ratings
• Increase revenues and profits 10 percent by end of the year	• Department Revenues • Department Net Profits	• Increase revenues and profits 10 percent by end of the year	• None
• Improve service quality to customers 10 percent by end of the year	• Percent Service Requests Completed on Time • Percent Service Requests Needing Rework	• Improve service quality to customers 10 percent by end of the year	• Percent Help Desk Calls Needing Rework • Percent Help Desk Calls Abandoned • Percent Help Desk Calls Closed First Call • Average Length of Help Desk Call
• Lower service quality costs by 10 percent by mid-year	• Service Center Expenses	• Lower help desk expenses by 15 percent by mid-year	• Help Desk Expenses • Help Desk Expenses per Employee
• Complete a needs analysis within 90 days	• Number of Skill Needs Identified	• Complete a needs analysis for help desk personnel within 90 days	• Number of Skill Needs Identified

Figure 6.1. *Sample Worksheet from the Help Desk Manager*

"Makes sense to me," Catherine said. "I'll put the department's revenues and profits on my scorecard if everyone does the same. We all need to contribute to the 10 percent improvements." Everyone agreed.

"I was wondering about your 'average length of help desk call,'" Anne said. "How does that help service quality?"

"It's a measure we've always tracked," Catherine said. "We argue every year whether we should shorten the call length for efficiency or make it longer to improve service. We don't know, but we always watch it."

"What about not tracking it on your scorecard?" Miguel asked. "Maybe it's useful to your supervisors and service specialists for feedback if the calls get too long, but how do you manage with it?"

Catherine thought for a moment, then answered, "I'd be willing to try that. I never know what to do with the results, anyway."

"Sounds like you're getting the hang of the vital few," Bob said. "Now, let's take a look at whether your measures are appropriate for your level."

> # Cascade
> ### Step 2
> Verify Cascaded Measures Are at the Appropriate levels

"What does that mean?" Anne asked.

"Most managers measure too many items, obscuring the vital few that provide insight to performance," Bob explained. "We avoid this by evaluating whether your scorecard contains the right measures for your organizational level."

Bob passed around a copy of the diagram shown in Figure 6.2. "Level of measure is defined by the terms M1, M2, M3, or M4—or even M5 or M6!" he explained.

Bob explained to the SolvNET managers, "M1 measures are company-level measures. They provide top-level managers a summary of performance from multiple areas, categories, or business units.

"For example, corporate expenses 'rolled up' for several business units is an M1 measure for financial performance. Each business unit's expense total represents an M2 measure."

"So my boss should use mostly M1 measures," Vince said.

"Right," Bob responded, "while you have mostly M2 measures. M2 measures are end-process measures that result from process outcomes. M2 measures relate to cross-functional processes that involve several groups in delivering service to the external customer. Typically, M2 measures are a composite of M3 measures."

Anne asked, "So, M2 measures are end-process measures—things like external customer satisfaction, total rework rates, or total cycle time?"

Bob grinned, "You got it!"

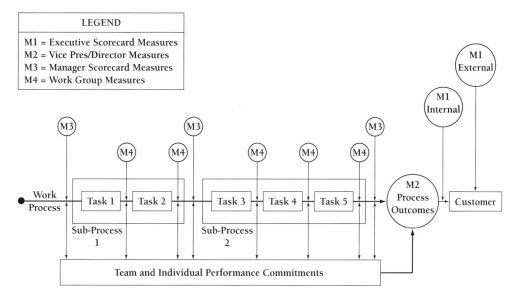

Figure 6.2. *Illustration of Measures Varying According to Organizational Level*

He continued, "M3 measures are sub-process measures. M3 measures result from sub-process outcomes that apply to a portion of the cross-functional process. M3 measures provide insight to the process 'gates.' How long did it take to get there? How much did it cost to arrive? How many errors are corrected before we proceed to the next gate?

"Typically, M3 measures are used by managers responsible for a portion of a larger process—just like you. An example of an M3 measure is the time from customer request to service order completion. As you expect, M3 measures result from combining M4 measures," Bob said.

Miguel interrupted, "Let me guess. M4 measures are parts of M3 measures. They measure pieces of the work process."

"You're getting the hang of it," Bob said. "M4 measures are functional or task-level measures. M4 measures reflect in-process activities or results from a manager or supervisor. These are the 'nuts and bolts' measures that teams use to make sure things run smoothly each day.

"The cycle time from customer request to technician dispatch is an M4 measure. Or, the time from technician dispatch to service order completion is an M4 measure. M5 and M6 measures provide details on M4 measures to support root-cause analysis or further breakdowns into categories.

"For example, the M4 measure of average time from customer request to technician dispatch may include M5 measures of cycle times for orders requiring parts and cycle times for orders not requiring parts," Bob said.

"As a manager, I wouldn't normally track M4 or M5 measures, but I could ask for the results to analyze a problem if I saw my M3 measure going haywire?" Max asked.

"That's right, Max," Bob said. "Normally your work group monitors the details. When things are cascaded properly, the work group members know that their results affect your results. So, work groups tend to be more proactive in monitoring and improving results."

Bob continued, "Drilling down one more layer, an M6 measure might include the types of system errors that are corrected. By tracking this level of detail at the operational level, faults can be monitored for appropriate preventive or corrective actions." Bob paused and looked around the room.

"OK, so what?" Anne asked. The entire team erupted with laughter.

"I figured that question was coming," Bob said. "Let's review Catherine's measures to see whether they are appropriate for a manager's level." The team looked at Catherine's list again, summarized below.

⇨ Customers' help desk ratings;

⇨ Customer services revenues;

⇨ Customer services net profits;

⇨ Percent help desk calls needing rework;

⇨ Percent help desk calls abandoned;

⇨ Percent help desk calls closed first call;

⇨ Help desk expenses;

⇨ Help desk expenses per employee; and

⇨ Number of skill needs identified.

"Quiz time," Bob announced. "What types of measures should Catherine have?"

"Well, from what you said, she's part of a bigger process. I'd say M3 measures, the ones that measure a sub-process area like the help desk," Miguel said.

"Very good," Bob said. "Do all of these look like M3 measures—part of bigger process measures?"

The group looked over the list. "I'd say so," Vince said. "Except for the customer services revenue and profits that we already discussed. Looks like she has them pretty well covered."

"Excellent," Bob said. "Catherine scores a big 10 for her draft measures. Catherine, how do you feel about these? Do you think you can manage to these vital few?"

Catherine thought for a moment, then replied, "As long as my supervisors and staff are tracking a lot of the details I now review. Yes, I'd be willing to give it a try."

The team applauded. "Great, now all of you will have a turn in the hot seat," Bob said.

"But, Bob, when do we determine the measures and level of detail that our work groups use?" Anne asked.

"Thanks, Anne, for introducing the next phase. That's exactly what we do in the Connect Phase, which we will cover next time. For now, let's make sure we have your scorecards right," Bob responded.

Cascade
Step 3
Establish and Affirm Linkages and Alignment

The team spent the rest of the afternoon going through the remaining managers' measures. They discovered that Miguel had too many measures—primarily at the M4 level. Anne needed some help with defining two of her indicators. Max seemed to struggle the most, but after seeing several examples and receiving help from the other managers, he developed a set of measures that suited his role as work station services manager.

"Very good," Bob said, "You've all done a great job with your scorecard drafts. Now, you need to verify your horizontal linkages, that is, check the linkages across your scorecards."

"Show us an example, Bob," Vince requested.

"Sure," Bob responded, "let's go back through the managers' scorecards and pick up measures that should link across the processes. Who can describe your service process at a high level?"

"That's easy," Miguel responded. "A customer calls with a problem, we fix the problem, and we close the problem."

"Thanks, Miguel," Bob said. "Now, the fix might include a work station repair, a network repair, or some other type of problem, right?"

"Sure," Anne said, "it could be anything from a password reset to a failure on the network. We fix them all."

"So, the fix step is subdivided according to the type of problem. What are your three main types of problems?" Bob asked.

"I would say a work station problem, a network problem, and a system problem," Anne said. "A system problem might be software related or caused by the network not recognizing a work station. Miguel and his technical integration team handle those."

"OK," Bob said, "let's put those into a table with the managers who are responsible for each area and see whether they have draft measures related to rework or defects within each area." Bob completed the table shown in Figure 6.3.

"We have a measure for each process step, so that's encouraging," Vince said. "But it looks as if we have a problem with consistency of measures and terms. I notice that some of the measures are percentages and others are numbers. Plus, we don't always call it rework. Is that how you see it, Bob?"

"Very good," Bob said. "You're right that you will need to align measurement units and terms, but this is a good start. Now, what about a roll-up measure for Vince? What would be on his scorecard?"

"Wouldn't it be as simple as the percent of service repairs needing rework that we identified already? Wouldn't the numbers from the help desk, work stations, network, and all sources roll into that measure?" Libby said.

"Very good," Bob said, "so, you need to look at your remaining measures across your business processes for linkages and consistency. Holly, do you think you can help with the summary and analysis for this step?"

"Sure, I think so," Holly said.

Process Step	Functional Area	Manager	Measure
Customer makes trouble call	Help Desk	Catherine	Percent Help Desk Calls Requiring Rework
Repair work station problem	Work Station Services	Max	Percent Work Station Repairs Needing to Be Reopened
Repair network problem	Network Services	Anne	Number of Network Service Orders Failing to Close First Time
Repair system problem	Technical Integration	Miguel	Number of System Work Orders Needing Rework
Close trouble call	Help Desk	Catherine	Percent Help Desk Calls Requiring Rework

Figure 6.3. *Possible Horizontal Linkages of Managers' Measures*

"Good, then we're ready to go on. Your next step is to develop targets for your scorecard measures. As you develop your management scorecard and define targets, you're likely to encounter the following questions from work teams," Bob said. He moved to the flip chart and wrote the following list:

⇨   How are targets set?

⇨   Is each target a minimum, average, or "stretch" goal to achieve?

⇨   What happens when we reach the target?

⇨   How long will we need to sustain the target when achieved?

⇨   Does every team have to achieve the same target?

⇨   Will the target value be averaged so that some teams are above and some below?

⇨   How often are targets updated?

"Spend the time now to clarify targets and issues involved in achieving them. Once everyone understands the targets, they are much easier to attain," Bob said. "Remember our discussion about targets when we developed Vince's scorecard? Who remembers the four sources for targets?"

"Statistical and historical results," Holly said.

"Customers' requirements," Miguel said.

"Industry standards and benchmarks," Anne said.

"The most demanding source of all, your boss," Max said, pointing to Vince. Everyone chuckled.

"Very good," Bob said. "All of those are correct. As you develop your new scorecard, you'll need to look closely at target values and the sources for those targets. We can't do that today, because you need to gather and review your baseline data first. But we'll discuss your baselines and your targets in our next meeting." The team members nodded approval.

"Great, let's look at our next step, to establish summary measures," Bob continued. "Your team keeps watch over daily details of performance with team and individual measures. At the management level, you monitor performance across many areas with your scorecard.

Cascade

Step 5

Establish Summary Measures, As Needed

"A summary measure, sometimes known as an *index,* helps you see results from many measures with a single value. Indexes, or indices, are used to monitor performance across several locations, teams, or processes.

"By examining individual measures, indices give you 'drill down' capabilities to pinpoint problem areas. Also, indexing aligns efforts throughout your organization, as relationships between measures and responsibilities are clarified. This is an effective management tool that reduces your time for reviewing performance while actually giving you a better overview of performance and empowering your team to take control of the daily measures.

"Last time you asked how we could combine customer satisfaction data. Let's look at an example that I put together from your customer satisfaction results," Bob suggested. He turned a page on the flip chart to reveal the chart shown in Figure 6.4.

"Wow," Catherine said, "this looks complicated."

"No, this is really very simple," Libby said. "Let Bob explain."

"An index allows us to combine measures that may not use the same units into one overall number," Bob said. "The key is to translate the numbers into a standard ten-point performance scale. For example, a 10 on the performance scale might equal a 90 percent help desk rating, a 4.0 rating for feedback cards, or a 10 from interview ratings."

"Oh, I get it," Vince said. "Every type of customer satisfaction measure is translated into a ten-point rating that we can average—or even do a weighted average."

Measure	Help Desk Ratings	Feedback Cards	Interview Results	Performance Scale	
	90 percent	4.0	10	10	Stretch Goal
	80 percent	3.9	9.5	9	
	70 percent	3.8	9.0	8	
	60 percent	3.7	8.5	7	Target
	50 percent	3.6	8.0	6	
Performance Range	40 percent	3.5	7.5	5	
	38 percent	3.4	7.0	4	
	36 percent	3.2	6.5	3	Baseline
	34 percent	3.0	6.0	2	
	32 percent	2.5	5.5	1	
	30 percent	2.0	5.0	0	Unacceptable
Latest Rating					
Performance Level Score					
Weight	40	40	20	Index Score	
Value					

Figure 6.4. *Sample Customer Satisfaction Index*

"Right," Bob said, "let's plug in the actual values and see how this turns out. Our actual help desk rating for May was 80 percent. According to this scale, that's a 9."

"What happens if we have an 85 percent or some number between the two points?" Max asked.

"Then you calculate the score or just take the closest number on the performance scale. For our example, we'll just take the closest number," Bob said. "What were the ratings for your feedback cards?"

Miguel consulted his notes. "For May, ratings were 3.7. That translates to a 7."

"Very good," Bob said.

"Interview results were 6.8. I guess we take the closest value, which is 4," Anne said.

"Great," Bob said, "you're catching on fast. Now, we take the values and multiply times the weights. We weight the measures because some measures 'count' more than others. In our example, I weighted the help desk ratings and the feedback cards equally at 40, with a 20 weight for the interview results because help desk and feedback cards cover more customers."

"Why do you distribute 100 points?" Anne asked.

"It really could be any number, but 100 is easy to use and understand," Bob replied.

"OK, so we have our performance scores and our weights. Now we just multiply them together?" Vince asked.

"Right, we multiply to find the weighted score of each," Bob said. His updated chart is shown in Figure 6.5.

"So we have a score of 720. What does that say?" Miguel asked.

"Well, what would we have if every one of the indicators maxed out on the scale with a ten for each indicator?" Bob asked.

Measure	Help Desk Ratings	Feedback Cards	Interview Results	Performance Scale	
	90 percent	4.0	10	10	Stretch Goal
	80 percent	3.9	9.5	9	
	70 percent	3.8	9.0	8	
	60 percent	3.7	8.5	7	Target
Performance Range	50 percent	3.6	8.0	6	
	40 percent	3.5	7.5	5	
	38 percent	3.4	7.0	4	
	36 percent	3.2	6.5	3	Baseline
	34 percent	3.0	6.0	2	
	32 percent	2.5	5.5	1	
	30 percent	2.0	5.0	0	Unacceptable
Latest Rating	80 percent	3.7	6.8		
Performance Level Score	9	7	4		
Weight	40	40	20	Index Score	
Value	360	280	80	720	

Figure 6.5. *Customer Satisfaction Ratings with Values Calculated*

"One thousand," Catherine replied. "I get it: A 720 says we did pretty well, but there's room for improvement. A 300 says we're just at baseline; 700 says we're at our target value. We should be concerned if we stay below 500. Hey, this is neat!"

"OK, this just might work," Vince said. "But we need to work out the details for the scales and the weights. Good start—are there other indexes we need?"

The team reviewed others and decided that the customer satisfaction index for Vince's scorecard was sufficient for now, and they began to see how their individual scorecards linked to Vince's.

"Let's continue with Step 6," Bob said. The team nodded concurrence.

| **Cascade** |
| **Step 6** |
| Refine Steps for Gathering, Reporting, and Reviewing Results |

"As each of you uses a scorecard and better understands how scorecards link together, you'll identify ways to improve your measures and your business performance," Bob said. "Refining measures goes hand-in-hand with improving business performance. Here are six things to consider as you refine your scorecards."

Bob turned another page on the flip chart and wrote the following list:

⇨   Do a gut check;

⇨   Routinely review measurement definitions and terms;

⇨   Conduct random audits;

⇨   Don't monitor too many indicators;

⇨   Don't monitor too few indicators; and

⇨   Drop obsolete measures.

"Hey, that first one, the gut check, sounds like a Vince term. Did he put you up to that?" Max said.

"No," Bob laughed, "it's a simple way to remember that you have to keep your measures in perspective. Use your intuition for how things are going to validate your measurement results. If you suspect things are improving, but the numbers don't show it, check definitions, performance scales, and other factors of how numbers are tabulated and reported. In the same way, if the numbers are moving up, but nothing has really changed, check for number inflation, shifting definitions, improperly recorded results, or other factors.

"That leads to the second item, to review measurement definitions routinely. You assume everyone interprets and defines a measure the same way, but you find a lot of confusion when you start checking. Define the measures in writing and check them from time to time. Make sure the definitions fit the results you need to track.

"Sometimes, you need to change a definition," Bob continued. " For example, one team I worked with defined service response time as the time from when a technician received a service order until the technician showed up at the customer site. They realized the need to change the definition to match the customer's perception. They started response time with the customer's call to the help desk."

Bob pointed to the third item on the list: Conduct random audits. "Occasionally, you need to check data sources and steps for compiling measures. Verify that measures are collected properly, data is complete, and that any data exceptions are handled correctly. Let people know that you expect the truth in your reports. Don't punish people for telling the truth, but don't condone any number 'fudging.'"

Bob continued, "The tendency to monitor too many indicators is strong—resist it. A good rule of thumb for the maximum number of measures on a single scorecard is twenty; if you are monitoring more than twenty indicators during a single review, you are watching too many items.

"Monitoring performance is like driving your car. There are a few indicators you watch closely and regularly: speed, fuel level, and engine revolutions. Others are watched less often, but are important: oil pressure, total miles, and engine temperature.

"If you watch every indicator of automobile performance—emissions content, voltages, brake fluid level, oil volume, tire wear, coolant temperature, and others—you cannot focus on your main job of driving! The same is true of business measurements. Use enough to know you are moving in the direction you want, but don't get bogged down doing more measuring than managing."

Bob pointed to the next item. "In the same way, don't monitor so few measures that you don't understand what is actually happening. If you drive and only watch your speed, you may run out of gas. This varies according to businesses, but experience confirms that six indicators is about as 'light' as a scorecard gets.

"The last one, 'drop obsolete measures,' is critical, but a hard one to do," Bob said. "As business needs change, your measurement needs change. Schedule regular reviews for the content of your scorecard. Drop indicators that don't give you meaningful insight to performance. Just because a measurement has always been around doesn't mean it tells you anything useful."

> **⇨ Expert Tip**
>
> Cascade outcomes:
> - A balanced and linked set of scorecard measures
> - Appropriate feedback measures for each level of accountability

"All of these will make more sense as you begin using your scorecards," Bob concluded. "I'm reviewing them with you now so that you understand that your scorecard and its measures will evolve as you, your team, and your business needs change. Remember that measures are only a tool to help you run your business. Change your tools to fit your business, not your business to fit your tools."

Bob paused and looked around the room: "You've done a good job of drafting your measures and being attentive to the actions you'll need to use them effectively. Looks like you're ready for the next step, to gather your data and begin your reviews. Any questions?"

No one on the team responded. "I'll take that to mean that you're ready. We'll check with each other at our next session to see how that's coming and prepare for our next step, to *connect* the scorecards to our employee's daily efforts. Our next review is two weeks away, and we'll be ready to do the Connect Phase at the meeting after that. See you next time!"

The team broke up and headed off. Vince pulled Bob aside and said, "I just want you to know that this is making a big difference. This is one of the first meetings in which my managers seemed to pull for each other and began to understand how they fit together to serve customers. Usually, there's a lot of finger pointing and posturing. But this scorecard stuff seems to help us work as a team."

"Thanks, Vince," Bob said. "That's one of many side benefits of scorecards. It's nice to know that you're getting that benefit. Let's keep going—there's more to come!"

"I'm with you," Vince said as he shook Bob's hand.

Summary

In the fourth phase, you *cascade* your Performance Scorecard measures to the next level of the organization, ensuring alignment with objectives and processes. During the cascade, you help front-line managers understand how progress toward business objectives is monitored with scorecard measures. Also, you help each manager relate team-level contributions to scorecard outcomes.

The Cascade Phase is done by completing the steps shown in the summary table below. This provides relevant feedback at the appropriate points in the organization for timely reviews and decisions while keeping your vital few scorecard measures aligned to your work teams' objectives and results.

PHASE	STEPS	OUTCOMES

Phase 4: CASCADE

1. Determine scorecard measures for next level in the cascade.	• A balanced and linked set of scorecard measures
2. Verify cascaded measures are at the appropriate levels.	• Appropriate feedback measures for each level of accountability
3. Establish and affirm linkages and alignment.	
4. Clarify targets.	
5. Establish summary measures, as needed.	
6. Refine steps for gathering, reporting, and reviewing results.	

Measurement Case Study: City of Indianapolis

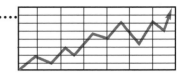

An APQC Measurement Case Study

It's rare that a city government is recognized for innovation and efficiency; the City of Indianapolis is an exception. Indianapolis was the first municipality to use private-sector business management principles to develop an aggressive public-sector performance management program. Now with a four-year track record of success and savings of nearly $100 million, Indianapolis is demonstrating the benefits that measurement and competition can bring to city government.

To support the turnaround, the city used five main initiatives:

⇨   Performance measures;

⇨   Performance reporting;

⇨   Performance-based compensation;

⇨   Activity-based costing (ABC) management; and

⇨   Activity-based/performance budgeting.

City leaders realized that many of their old performance measures did not measure the right outcomes. For example, there's a big difference between measuring how many tons of garbage were picked up in a year and the number of customer complaints. The first big initiative was to change the focus of what was measured.

⇨   Performance measures were restructured so that they could be understood by the citizens, council members, and employees alike.

⇨   They stopped using meaningless measures, such as tracking people and resources. Instead, they focused on what was accomplished through people and resources.

⇨   They launched a comprehensive ABC training effort to promote a "measurement mentality" and built it into their employee orientation.

Getting the word out was an integral part of promoting Indianapolis' continuous improvement culture.

➪ A variety of media sources were used to provide city staff members with detailed performance information and its public constituencies with more broad-based highlights.

➪ Departmental models tracked basic ABC information for managers and the mayor. The models were updated regularly and issued in reports providing information on equipment, vehicle and material usage, measures against the plan, and labor statistics.

➪ Key indicators and results—whether good news or bad—were posted on employee bulletin boards and discussed in weekly departmental meetings.

➪ Citizens were able to view key accomplishments on the city's website or watch city leaders on a controlled-access television channel discussing and planning for greater efficiency.

➪ Several city divisions greatly increased the number of face-to-face neighborhood meetings used to explain projects and listen to residents' concerns. One noteworthy example was the Indianapolis Fleet Services Division, which increased customer meetings from 32 to 192 a year.

To overcome the hurdle of employee resistance, employees were trained how to measure quality, efficiency, and productivity using activity-based management (ABM). Employees saw, for the first time, how the cost of activities they performed could be determined—and how improvements could impact those costs.

Another hurdle was getting the union on board. Union relations had traditionally been rocky at best, but in a surprisingly short time relations improved dramatically. The union joined management as a "partner" to determine ways to cut costs.

The Department of Transportation (DOT) used activity-based costing to examine its operations. Initial numbers revealed that its mix of equipment and labor was grossly inefficient. The Department of Transportation determined it could repair a pothole with four workers instead of eight and with one truck instead of two. This was an important early victory. It proved once and for all that government could be as efficient as the private sector when city managers had the right incentives and tools to think like entrepreneurs.

Employees were rewarded with a new incentive payment structure tied to performance management goals. This public-sector "profit sharing" program contributed to employee buy-in from the once-resistant workforce. A city administrator agreed, "Paying employees a bonus when targets are surpassed has a tremendous effect on morale. It's also had a profound impact on a positive culture and attitude change."

Indianapolis is open about its success secrets: Do the research, put new systems in place, set up better measurements, and promote the good news. Competition has brought a new efficiency to the city's operation:

⇨ Costs are down 29 percent;

⇨ Turnaround time on repairs has improved significantly; and

⇨ Customer complaints have fallen more than 90 percent.

Employees have prospered in the climate of competition. *Time* magazine reported that they "have more than made up for their lost raises, averaging 5 percent salary hikes in each of the past four years—well above the city average."

Downsizing was an inevitable outcome of increased efficiency. But as in everything, the city gave it careful consideration. Workforce reductions were accomplished over time to prevent lapses in productivity and progress. In one division alone, the number of managers was reduced from 19 to eight as groups became streamlined and self-managed.

The city openly shares the lessons learned from its improvement experience:

⇨ Output quantity is easier to measure than outcome quality, but both are equally important.

⇨ At first your tendency is to make your list of "what to measure" too long, but over time the important measures will surface.

➪ Training must permeate all employee groups to realize true grass-roots changes.

➪ Never get comfortable with your competitive position, because you never know what your opponent will do next.

➪ Empower and trust your employees to make decisions and be accountable for their results.

Indianapolis leaders have reason to be proud of the city government and its employees' accomplishments. They've become creative in reducing costs and burdensome regulations, and they've created a vibrant city that encourages economic development and retains regional competitiveness.

One official acknowledges that the changes are everywhere, " . . . from roads that have been resurfaced to clean and safer neighborhoods. We have increased economic development, revitalized the inner city, and have a new athletic facility—all without a tax increase."

"Aggressive Performance Management and Measurement Pay Off: City of Indianapolis Pioneers Privatization," by April Canik; *Measurement in Practice* (October/November 1997) *Issue 10*, Houston, TX: American Productivity & Quality Center (APQC) © 1997. Reprinted with permission. Contact APQC for full text.

CHAPTER 7

Connect Your Scorecard

In this chapter, Vince works with his managers to cascade the measures to individual employees, helping connect management scorecards with performance plans, objectives, and measures for individuals. Vince uses SolvNET's performance management process to link individual commitments to scorecard results, helping to reinforce key business outcomes.

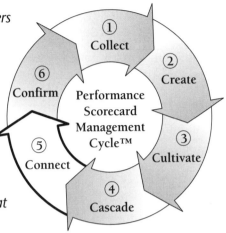

During the Connect Phase, Vince realizes that his earlier frustrations over results are felt through all levels of his department. As scorecards are discussed and developed at the employee level, issues of ownership, collaboration, process ownership, and target clarity are surfaced and resolved. A greater capability for collaboration, problem solving, and alignment toward goals begins to emerge.

Vince and his managers had been using their scorecards for nearly four months and were pleased with their progress. They could more easily track progress toward business objectives and take quicker and more direct actions to treat problems.

Connect

Steps

1. Review Your Performance Management Process
2. Develop an Individual Performance Plan
3. Conduct Coaching Sessions
4. Provide Evaluation Summaries
5. Review Links and Outcomes

With the help of their improved measures, Vince's managers felt that the easy problems had been identified and addressed. Results were improving, and trends were starting to move in the right direction. But the managers felt a sense of "hitting a wall" for making additional improvements. They sensed there were additional improvements to make, but saw that continued improvements would be a more difficult.

Bob called Vince to check in before the next regularly scheduled review. Vince shared with Bob his managers' feeling of success and their concerns over continuing their momentum.

"Good, you're ready for the next phase, *connect,*" said Bob.

"You'll need to help me, Bob," Vince said. "We connected the managers' scorecards to my scorecard and aligned their scorecards. My scorecard is connected to Jan Larson's measures and SolvNET strategy. What's left?"

"You have to connect the managers' scorecards to employees' performance objectives," Bob said. "Measures link SolvNET strategies with the daily work of front-line employees. That way, you monitor daily progress toward strategic objectives. Using the connect process, you help each employee understand how he or she contributes to the overall success of your organization and the importance of the vital few measures. This keeps your team focused on key outcomes for your business."

"Sounds like the right thing to keep our momentum going," Vince said.

"To start the Connect Phase, tell me more about your performance management process," Bob said. "Do you have a system to develop individual performance plans and coach employees toward objectives?"

Vince paused to think, "Sure, but we never really related them to our measures. It's just our way to get employee development information and pump up morale."

Bob chuckled, "That's the reaction I usually get. Most businesses don't relate performance management with measures."

Vince and Bob discussed SolvNET's performance management process and the following week's regularly scheduled review, at which time they would cover the Connect Phase.

The next week, Bob reviewed the latest results during the team's normal business review and commended the members for their results. They appeared a little more upbeat than usual.

"Our team feels an initial rush of success," Vince said, "but we recognize that we have a long way to go. From what we discussed, it looks as if we're ready for the Connect Phase. Tell us more."

"SolvNET performance is linked to individual performance," Bob said. "To reach your business targets, individual efforts must tie to team objectives and scorecards. But this doesn't mean that you break down every scorecard measure into individual measures. You leave many measures at the team level and help each individual understand how his or her efforts contribute to team results."

Bob continued, "Deploying team-level objectives and measures to individuals is commonly done using a performance management process. Your performance management process is straightforward, with planning sessions between employees and

> **Connect**
>
> **Step 1**
>
> Review Your Performance
> Management Process

managers with at least one interim review and a year-end review." The managers nodded.

Bob referred to the diagram on his flip chart, shown in Figure 7.1. "Here's an illustration of SolvNET's performance management process, typical of most organizations. Let's look at the three main steps of performance management: *planning, coaching,* and *evaluating.*"

"During the planning step, you and each employee jointly develop an individual performance plan," Bob continued. "The plan establishes objectives, commitments, and expectations."

> **Connect**
>
> **Step 2**
>
> Develop an Individual
> Performance Plan

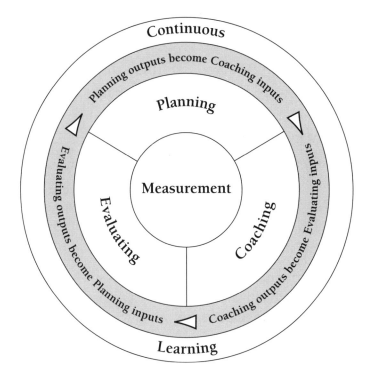

Figure 7.1. *Connecting Scorecard Measures to Employee Performance*

"Right, Bob," Anne said, "it works pretty well if we're conscientious and follow through with the steps."

"Good," Bob said, "it's a real plus that you managers do this now. It makes the Connect Phase that much easier. For connect, you prepare for the planning session with employees by assembling the following." Bob referred to the flip chart.

⇨ SolvNET's operational plans, including business goals and customers' requirements;

⇨ Customer Services' objectives;

⇨ Customer Services' scorecard;

⇨ Departmental action plans; and

➱	Each employee's current job description, responsibilities, and objectives.

"As you look at the employee's current job description, responsibilities, and objectives, consider the following questions," Bob said as he wrote on the flip chart.

➱	What aspects of the job must be completed by this employee for your team to accomplish its objectives?

➱	How much can this employee influence the outcome of this objective?

➱	What commitments should be assigned to achieve department and team plans?

➱	How will these commitments be measured? That is, how do they link to the measures on your team's scorecard?

Bob continued, "Next, you draft the individual performance plan that includes key commitments and measures. Key commitments are employee-level objectives that identify the individual's outcomes that support business plans. Key commitments focus on team objectives and, ultimately, scorecard measures."

"So, key commitments are the important things the employee must do for the team to succeed?" Catherine asked.

"Exactly," Bob said as he wrote on the flip chart. "Here are characteristics of key commitments."

Key commitments should:

➱	Focus on the most critical elements of the job;

➱	Specify desired outcomes and associated measures; and

➱	Be within the employee's influence or control.

Bob said, "Key commitments include challenging assignments beyond normal job responsibilities. Opportunities to develop employees' skills and team capabilities are defined with key commitments."

"What if I want an employee to complete project management certification? Is that an appropriate key commitment?" Miguel said.

"That sounds like a key commitment as long as it's tied to a business objective, such as 'develop a project team environment.' Here are a few more characteristics of key commitments," Bob said as he flipped the page and wrote on the flip chart again.

Well-written key commitments are:

➪ Focused on results/outcomes;

➪ Specific;

➪ Based on customer expectations;

➪ Time-based;

➪ Realistic, achievable—within the employee's control to accomplish; and

➪ Measurable, that is, linked to the measures on your team's scorecard.

"How about some examples, Bob, to help us see how they link to team objectives and measures?" Vince asked.

"Thanks, Vince, for introducing my prepared chart," Bob grinned as he turned to the next flip-chart page.

"Let's use Catherine's scorecard as our example with a connection to one of her employees on the help desk," Bob said. "Here's a table to show how they fit together." Bob referred to the chart shown in Figure 7.2.

Help Desk Team Objective	Help Desk Team Scorecard Measure	Employee Key Commitment	Individual Measure
Increase customer satisfaction by 10 percent	Customers' Help Desk Ratings	Chair a team to review and refine the problem resolution process	Customers' Help Desk Ratings

Figure 7.2. *Sample Key Commitments for a Help Desk Employee*

"In this case," Bob continued, "the employee's measure is the same as the team's measure. We want the employee to improve the problem resolution process with results toward customers' help desk ratings."

"Wouldn't you give the employee a more direct measure for the key commitment, such as the cycle time for the problem resolution process?" Anne asked.

"You could," Bob explained, "but be careful that you don't obtain a suboptimal result. If you only shorten cycle time for resolving problems, you may generate more dissatisfied customers because resolutions are rushed and incomplete. The attempt here is to improve the process with gains in satisfaction, so that's the measure you'll link to improvement efforts."

Bob continued, "Here's another example in which you may have an individual employee measure because the key commitment is unique to the employee." Bob referred to a chart shown in Figure 7.3.

Help Desk Team Objective	Help Desk Team Scorecard Measure	Employee Key Commitment	Individual Measure
Improve service quality to customers 10 percent by end of the year	Percent Help Desk Calls Needing Rework	Reduce rework calls associated with software trouble calls	Percent Software Trouble Calls Needing Rework

Figure 7.3. *Employee Measure Linked to Help Desk Scorecard*

"So, the individual measure is part of the overall measure of calls needing rework?" Miguel asked.

"That's right," Bob said. "In this case, the employee is focused on the subset of trouble calls from software problems. You and the employee want to see whether efforts improve performance in this specific measure."

"The main thing," Bob continued, "is to see how the employee's key commitments link to the team scorecard measures. Sometimes the employee needs an individual scorecard, but that's rare. You want the employees to use the team scorecard as much as possible. Employees should understand how their key commitments tie to the team scorecard and keep things oriented to a team approach. Individual statistics are nice, but the entire team has to win."

"Here's the form you use for SolvNET's performance management process," Bob said as he passed around papers to the team. "I drafted an example to show you how everything connects." Bob's example is shown in Figure 7.4.

"For SolvNET's individual performance plans, there are four types of objectives: performance improvement, personal development, team development, or business development," Bob said. "Target dates define completion dates for key commitments. Associated measures define the measure for the manager's scorecard, the work group scorecard, or the individual's scorecard that relates to the key commitment."

"Wait, Bob, I'm getting confused. Are there actually three scorecards in the Connect Phase? My scorecard, a team scorecard, and individual scorecards?" Catherine asked.

"Maybe," Bob said with a smile. "It depends on the individual's skills, job responsibilities, and key commitments. If you have employees who have very different responsibilities with little overlap in their jobs, you may have individual scorecards for each employee. An example might include a team of project managers with individual projects. You use similar measures, such as project completion, project success, and business outcomes, but each project manager's scorecard is unique."

Individual Performance Plan

Employee: Susan Lee	Position: Supervisor, Help Desk Operations	Department: Customer Services Help Desk	Supervisor: Catherine Miller

Key Commitments	Type of Objective	Target Date	Associated Measure(s)
Complete Help Desk process analysis and implement improvements	Performance Improvement	2/1/XX	Percent Help Desk Calls Abandoned
Complete installation and training for knowledge management software	Performance Improvement	4/1/XX	Percent Help Desk Calls Closed First Call
Implement contact standards for customer service representatives	Team Development	6/1/XX	Customers' Help Desk Ratings
Train customer service representatives for "add-on" sales during routine calls	Financial	8/1/XX	Customer Services' Revenues
Complete management development series for "world class services"	Personal Development	4/1/XX	Percent Help Desk Calls Needing Rework
Implement at least 25 cost-saving employee suggestions	Financial	12/31/XX	Help Desk Expenses

Figure 7.4. *Sample Individual Performance Plan*

"Sure, I have a couple of specialized engineers who own projects that no one else can do," Miguel said. "Sounds like they might need individual scorecards."

"Right," Bob said. "On the other hand, if your employees have identical jobs, say telephone operators, you may not have any individual scorecards. They use a team-level scorecard because they contribute to overall team performance."

"Like the service specialists on the help desk," Catherine said. "They all do similar work of handling incoming calls, so they should use a single team-level scorecard."

"Right again," Bob said. "Sometimes you don't know whether you need individual scorecards or a team scorecard until you have planning discussions with employees. After your one-on-one sessions with employees, review the outcomes to see whether you need individual scorecards or a team-level scorecard. As always, focus on the vital few."

Connect **Step 3** Conduct Coaching Sessions

"When you've worked through the key commitments and measures, continue with coaching sessions throughout the year," Bob continued. "Remember, you are using scorecards to provide feedback regularly. Your chances of keeping on track with your objectives and targets improve with your use of feedback."

"Here are some other good reasons to provide ongoing feedback," Bob said as he wrote on the next flip-chart page.

➪ Builds a foundation of communication, trust, and respect;

➪ Keeps performance moving in a positive direction day-to-day;

➪ Clarifies expectations about performance levels, priorities, and responsibilities;

➪ Corrects inappropriate actions immediately; and

➪ Helps prevent surprises during final performance reviews.

"Lots of informal feedback is good, but you should do at least one formal coaching session during the year. During a coaching session, evaluate, discuss, and document the employee's performance toward achieving key commitments. If you've linked your measures correctly, you'll have charts and measurable feedback to give the employee. Address problems and developmental needs and, if necessary, make adjustments to the employee's individual performance plan," Bob said.

"For the fourth step of the Connect Phase, conduct year-end performance reviews to assess how well your employees contributed to the key commitments and scorecard targets," Bob said.

Connect
Step 4
Provide Evaluation Summaries

"Use the session to provide honest and constructive feedback on positive and negative aspects of performance. Help the employee see his or her contribution and the impact on scorecard measures. The stronger connection you make now, the more likely you'll be able to achieve your targets in the next planning and performance cycle," Bob said.

"So the evaluation sessions lead right into bonuses and promotions, right, Bob?" Vince asked. "After all, we have all the hard data from the scorecard to make compensation decisions."

"Not so fast, Vince," Bob replied. "You want to tie performance to pay at some point. But don't rush it. If you immediately link your scorecard with compensation, you may obtain inflated numbers that simply support the bonus plan but don't give you the truth about performance. Or people will resist measuring because bonuses could be jeopardized."

"What's the answer then?" Vince asked.

"Let people know that you plan to link compensation to measures after a pilot period, usually several months," Bob answered. "This gives people a chance to see how the measures perform and how they can influence results. Also, you want to make sure you have the right measures linked to performance. Sometimes, you get results you never intended by measuring the wrong thing."

Vince nodded, "I see that we would want to take a few months to work out any bugs before linking scorecards with compensation. Also, we want people to be comfortable with the measures, so we shouldn't hurry the compensation issue. Let's agree that we'll revisit it in three months to see whether our work groups are ready."

"But I want to get started with cascading right away," Vince continued. "We just received the notice to complete individual performance plans with all our employees within the next thirty days. Let's work on some specific examples, have the managers do their sessions with employees, and report back at our next regular monthly review on how the sessions went."

Bob agreed, "That's a wonderful way for managers to work through the Connect Phase. The only way to learn it is to do it!"

The managers worked together for the next two hours to draft and refine individual performance plans for employees. The managers realized that most employees easily connected to the managers' scorecards and measures, with a few exceptions of employees who required individual scorecards.

Max, the work station services manager, was intrigued to see whether the scorecard discussion could turn around a problem area on his team. One of his supervisors, Joan Betters, was having difficulty with her work group preparing work stations for installation.

Several times, the installation crew was delayed because Joan's work group had not done a thorough job of installing and checking out the software loads. Max was beginning to see the declining results with increased costs, fewer on-time installations, and decreasing customer satisfaction scores.

Max drafted an individual performance plan for Joan, shown in Figure 7.5.

Max arranged a meeting and reviewed the draft with Joan. Max also shared results from his work station installation scorecard, noting declining performance in

Individual Performance Plan

Employee:
Joan Betters

Position:
Supervisor, Work Station Staging

Department:
Customer Services Work Station Installation

Supervisor:
Max McFarland

Key Commitments	Type of Objective	Target Date	Associated Measure(s)
Complete work station staging and preparations according to specifications and work schedules	Performance Improvement	2/1/XX	Percent Work Stations Installed on Time; Work Station Installation Customer Satisfaction Ratings
Complete upgrades to staging lab equipment and facilities	Performance Improvement	4/1/XX	Percent Work Stations Installed on Time; Employee Satisfaction
Complete management development sessions on process management and supervisory skills	Personal Development	6/1/XX	Percent Work Station Installations Needing Rework; Employee Satisfaction
Reduce staging lab expenses by 10 percent	Financial	8/1/XX	Work Station Installation Expenses
Evaluate new work station models and propose enhanced customer solutions with greater effectiveness at reduced costs	Performance Improvement	4/1/XX	Work Station Installation Customer Satisfaction Ratings; Customer Services Revenues

Figure 7.5. *Individual Performance Plan for Work Station Services Supervisor*

work station installation customer satisfaction ratings, expenses, and on-time installations.

Joan seemed surprised by the declines and readily agreed to take action to address the problems. She expressed concern over expense reductions, claiming she couldn't see how to accomplish that objective, but said that she would try. She felt that all of the other key commitments fit her developmental and performance needs and welcomed the use of measurable feedback.

Joan and Max discussed other commitments related to personal development, employee development, and service center performance. The commitments and associated measures were documented on the individual performance plan and signed by Joan. They agreed to the date for the interim review and concluded their meeting with a handshake.

At Vince's next staff meeting, Max described his meeting with Joan. He was amazed at how well it had gone. He was already seeing improved results from Joan's work group. More work stations were ready on time, and Joan's team was carefully monitoring its measurement and working on ways to improve results.

> **Connect**
>
> **Step 5**
> Review Links and Outcomes

"As I completed the performance plans with all my supervisors, I realized they didn't have the feedback they needed," Max said. "Every one was surprised that we were having problems. I took for granted that they knew about these problems. Every supervisor responded favorably and was eager to receive the data."

"I also summarized the outcomes from all the supervisors and saw that I needed to make a couple of tweaks to my scorecard," Max continued. "I had a couple of measures that belonged to my supervisors and needed another summary measure for rolling up work station installation volume."

"Good job, Max," Bob said. "Did all of you experience the same thing?"

The managers nodded and shared similar stories of their managers and work groups being "feedback deprived."

"That's not surprising," Bob said. "Most people want the accountability and responsibility, but resist it because they don't know how they will be measured and what their targets are for success. Scorecards clear away that fog and help people take ownership of measures and performance. When they do that, you're ready to link compensation, because now they feel they can control the outcomes and drive performance to desired levels. Your team is really on a roll, Vince."

Vince smiled. "I know," he said.

Summary

In the Connect Phase, you connect scorecard measures to front-line employees, aligning scorecards with team objectives and individual performance plans. During the Connect Phase, you help each employee understand how progress is monitored with scorecard measures.

Using individual plans, coaching sessions, and evaluation summaries, you help each employee relate individual contributions to scorecard outcomes and business results. This builds ownership, acceptance, and responsibility for performance as employees begin to relate their efforts to the "vital few." This also lays a foundation for linking pay for performance after a period to allow employees to track and use measures within their work groups.

PHASE	STEPS	OUTCOMES
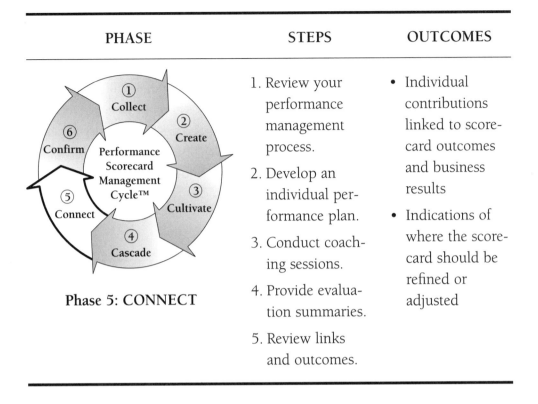 **Phase 5: CONNECT**	1. Review your performance management process. 2. Develop an individual performance plan. 3. Conduct coaching sessions. 4. Provide evaluation summaries. 5. Review links and outcomes.	• Individual contributions linked to scorecard outcomes and business results • Indications of where the scorecard should be refined or adjusted

Measurement Case Study: Texas Nameplate Company

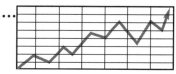

Texas Nameplate Company (TNC) makes nameplates, the small metal tags with etched letters that are riveted to refrigerators, computers, high-pressure valves, and military equipment. A small, privately held company in Dallas since 1946, you wouldn't think that a company like TNC would receive much attention. But as a winner of the 1998 Malcolm Baldrige National Quality Award, the 1997 Texas Business of the Year, and the 1996 Texas Quality Award, it is receiving more than a fair share of business press for a company with only 60 people.

The requirement to eliminate product defects came from a major customer, but then became a way of life. To achieve near perfection, TNC organized its business and measures around seven key result areas: employee satisfaction, fair profit, environmental consciousness, controlled growth, customer satisfaction, process organization, and external interface.

By focusing on a vital few measures in these areas (sales, margins, total nonconformances, customer nonconformances, revenues per production employee, on-time delivery, and cycle time for order completion), TNC made significant gains. Total orders jumped from approximately 6,000 per year in 1994 to nearly 9,000 in 1998. Gross profits as a percent of sales increased from 50.5 percent to 59 percent during the same period, and net profits more than doubled. TNC raised market share from 2.7 percent to 5.1 percent. Revenue per production employee went from about $66,000 in 1993 to an estimated $113,000 in 1998.

To engage the front line, TNC set a tough standard: Products are shipped defect free and on time or the order is free. In 1998, TNC eliminated its quality control department, putting responsibility with the Daily Operations Innovation Team (DOIT). Through the DOIT, supervisors are charged with sharing information and results with floor-level employees. Troy Knowlton, TNC operations manager, has said, "People on the floor can figure out what's happening and make adjustments the fastest. People on the floor are quick to help out when one person is having a problem. Information, once it gets into the hands of line employees, makes the biggest difference in driving down nonconformances."

The front line responded to the challenge: Over the last five years, only four orders have been free. Quality improvements cut in half the volume of over-runs necessary to offset rejected products, falling from 8 percent of outputs in 1993 to 4 percent today. Daily nonconformance results are posted and linked to gain-sharing with quarterly payouts when nonconformance rates are less than 5 percent. Payouts to date exceed $200,000, an average of $1.26 per hour for each employee. "We took four years to get our measurements in place," CEO Dale Crownover said. "If you start a gain-sharing plan without good measurements, you're going to give away money you don't have." He added, "The defect-free policy is a mind-set. It's a commitment we made to our people and our customers. It has proven to be a worthy goal for us. People are working at higher performance levels."

"Texas Nameplate Company: All You Need Is Trust" by Brad Stratton. *Quality Progress* (October 1998). Milwaukee, WI: American Society for Quality. Copyright © 1998 American Society for Quality. Reprinted with Permission.

"Making the Pitch in the Executive Suite: How Quality Got to the Top with Six Baldrige Award Winners" by Susan E. Daniels and Mark R. Hagen. *Quality Progress* (April 1999). Milwaukee, WI: American Society for Quality. Copyright © 1999 American Society for Quality. Reprinted with Permission.

Baldrige National Quality Program (January 1999). *Board of Examiners Update.* Gaithersburg, MD: National Institute of Standards and Technology.

CHAPTER 8

Confirm Your Scorecard

After several months of refinements, Vince and his management team review and confirm their scorecards to give more accurate and meaningful feedback. As they refine their measures, they reflect on issues about measurement process and content. They complete the final phase of the scorecard development cycle with a plan and process to keep scorecards current as business needs change.

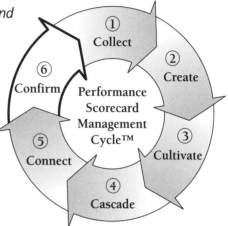

Vince's management team was celebrating at its monthly performance review. This was a special occasion, as the team was recognizing the six-month "anniversary" of Vince's scorecard. The team had invited Bob as its special guest.

The meeting was ready to start. Vince said, "All right, Holly, let's look at the latest." Holly turned on the electronic projector and displayed the entire scorecard, shown in Figure 8.1.

"It's good to see our customer satisfaction index up from last month," Vince said.

Confirm

Steps
1. Evaluate Your Scorecard
2. Prioritize and Act on Improvements
3. Identify and Resolve Measurement Issues
4. Establish a Process to Refine Your Scorecard Continually

"Yes," Catherine said, "the help desk ratings are up, feedback card ratings are slightly up, but interview results were actually the same."

"Thanks, Catherine, that's helpful to remind us of the index measures and a little detail," Vince said.

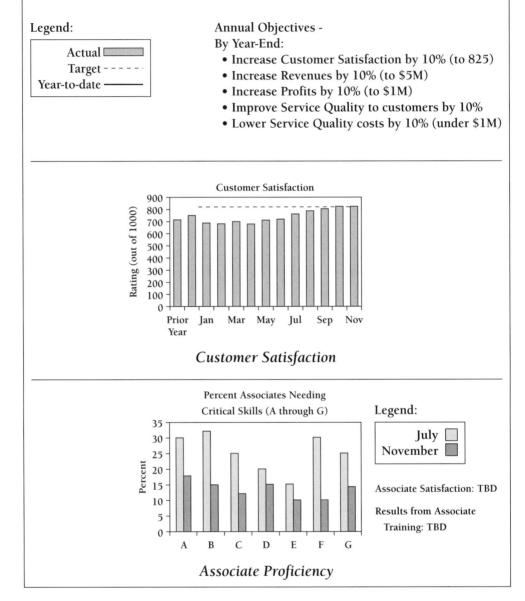

SolvNET
Customer Services Performance Scorecard

Legend:

Actual
Target - - - - -
Year-to-date ——————

Annual Objectives -
By Year-End:
- Increase Customer Satisfaction by 10% (to 825)
- Increase Revenues by 10% (to $5M)
- Increase Profits by 10% (to $1M)
- Improve Service Quality to customers by 10%
- Lower Service Quality costs by 10% (under $1M)

Customer Satisfaction

Customer Satisfaction

Percent Associates Needing
Critical Skills (A through G)

Legend:

July
November

Associate Satisfaction: TBD

Results from Associate
  Training: TBD

Associate Proficiency

Figure 8.1. *SolvNET's Customer Services Scorecard After Six Months*

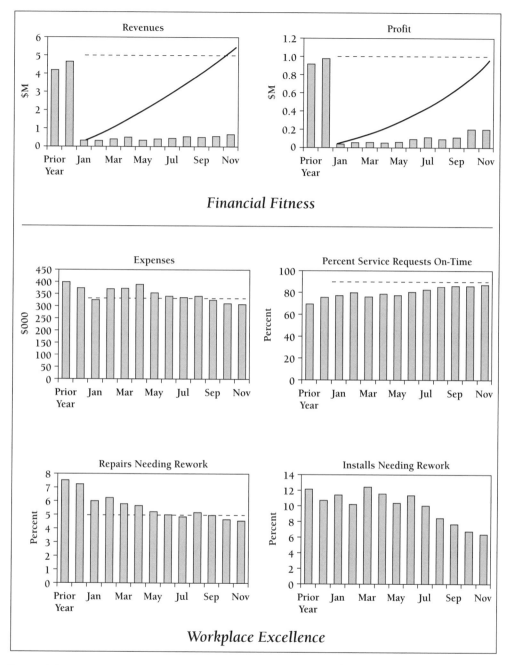

Figure 8.1. *Continued*

"Hey, look at our revenues and profits," Miguel said. "What's causing the good news?"

"It looks like several factors," Vince said. "I believe sharing the results with our entire team across all of our functions is making our people more conscious of sales. Also, we're seeing initiatives at the front-line levels to trim expenses. I think people enjoy knowing what's important to the business and seeing their efforts turn into measurable results."

"Looks like the same factors are working with the percent of service requests completed on time and the requests needing rework," Max said. "My guys have really been working to make sure we get them done on time and get them done right. They're talking regularly with the help desk folks and the sales team to make sure we have the information we need to get the cases completed. They're excited."

"Max, that is fantastic. Looks like we need to take another look at our target because they're going to beat it soon," Vince said.

"We're ahead of you there, Vince," Holly said. "We've started to do some benchmarking to determine best performers in our industry and see where we might need to reset our target."

"This just keeps getting better," Vince said.

"We're making progress on the results from the needs analysis, too," Holly said. "We're working with the training group to make sure that our folks have the critical skills that we identified from the survey. We're closing some skill gaps, but still have some work to finish in this area."

"Great, and I see you left a spot for the measures we discussed in our last review, the 'associate satisfaction' and 'results from training.' Good job, Holly," Vince said.

The team continued its discussion for a few minutes, noting the positive trends for every measure and discussing reasons for the turnaround and the reactions from work groups. Overall, feedback from employees was enthusiastic; they liked scorecards. Measurable results were turning around, and areas not currently measured, such as morale and employee involvement, were noticeably improving. It appeared that the meeting was about to conclude as everyone slipped into side conversations.

"Vince, you and your team have done a great job of developing your scorecards," Bob said, "but don't get too carried away with your celebration. You have one more phase to complete, *confirm*."

"Confirm?" Vince asked. "Look at the numbers and talk with our employees. Sure, we have a ways to go in some areas, but we're pretty happy with our results so far."

"I'm happy that you're pleased, but what about some of the lingering questions that I heard during the review?" Bob said. "There are still a couple of holes in your scorecard, and it doesn't look like the managers have addressed all the issues with their scorecards. Also, you have to consider how to manage changes to your scorecard. You were talking earlier about adding new services and systems. How will you measure those areas?"

Vince looked at Bob soberly, "You're right; we need to finish the job we started. It just felt so good to see things turn around."

"You're never done with your scorecard," Bob said. "As long as your business changes, your scorecard will need to change to stay in alignment."

The rest of the team turned from their side conversations to Bob. "What's left to do?" Miguel asked.

Bob explained, "The final phase of the scorecard development process, Confirm, has four steps. Even when you're done with Confirm, you're not finished with your scorecard. You have to remain alert to business changes that affect your measures. These might include changes to products, services, processes, organizational structure, objectives, targets, or other areas. Your scorecard is rarely static. If your business changes dramatically, you may need to start the entire scorecard development cycle again."

"Tell us about the steps for the Confirm Phase," Anne said. "How do we keep our scorecards current?"

"The steps are simple," Bob said. "More importantly, you need to be ready to tackle issues that will pop up as you improve your measures. Let me take you through the confirm steps and then give you tips for handling measurement issues and establishing a process for routinely managing scorecard changes."

Bob passed around handouts for each manager. "The six-month anniversary is a good opportunity to evaluate your scorecard. Your handout contains a scorecard evaluation and some tips for managing issues. I would recommend completing this survey every six to twelve months to evaluate your scorecards and point out issues for keeping them current."

Bob continued, "Take a look at the survey, which assesses three primary areas:

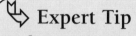 **Expert Tip**

Confirm outcomes
- Scorecard assessment
- Scorecard improvement strategies and plans
- Improved scorecards

⇨ Scorecard Alignment;

⇨ Scorecard Processes; and

⇨ Scorecard Content.

"Here's an opportunity for you to assess your primary tool for measuring and managing performance candidly, so be honest. The results will only be known to you and will help you pinpoint weaknesses in your scorecard."

"Do you want us to fill these out now?" Max asked.

"Yes, and fill them out for your specific scorecard and your specific team. Your team is defined as your unit of responsibility, whether it is a work group, department, or area under your span of control," Bob explained. "Complete each section and rate each statement using the five-point scale provided. At the end, tally and interpret your results."

Bob explained the survey rating scale and gave the managers fifteen minutes to complete the survey, which is shown on the next page.

Section A: Assessing Scorecard Alignment

Read each of the following statements. For each, rate the degree to which your measures are aligned with your business strategies based on the following response scale:

5 = Strongly Agree   2 = Disagree
4 = Agree   1 = Strongly Disagree
3 = Neither Agree nor Disagree

Section A: Scorecard Alignment	Rating (5 to 1)
1. Our scorecard helps us focus on our team's business objectives.	
2. Our team's objectives and measures are linked to our corporate goals and strategic priorities.	
3. Our team's objectives, measures, and targets are linked to our customers' requirements.	
4. Our scorecard measures promote understanding of overall company strategies within our team.	
5. Customers' requirements are used for determining team objectives and measures.	
6. Objectives and measures that link to our suppliers are identified and tracked.	
7. We set clear and appropriate performance targets for our team's scorecard measures.	
8. Our team's scorecard measures allow us to identify clear improvement objectives.	
9. The right people from our team are informed and involved throughout scorecard and measurement development.	
10. The right people from our suppliers, customers, and associated processes are involved with our scorecard development process.	
Subtotal:	

Section B: Assessing Scorecard Processes

Read each of the following statements. For each statement, rate your team's success with developing and using your scorecard, using the following scale:

5 = Strongly Agree 2 = Disagree

4 = Agree 1 = Strongly Disagree

3 = Neither Agree nor Disagree

Section B: Scorecard Processes	Rating (5 to 1)
11. Tracking and evaluating our scorecard is efficient, with minimal paperwork and administrative overhead.	
12. Our scorecard measures are appropriate for our area of business responsibility and control.	
13. Managers and employees are held accountable for measurement accuracy and performance results.	
14. Following reviews, scorecard results are acted on in a timely way.	
15. Performance targets are based on the actual and desired capabilities of our systems.	
16. Scorecard measurement data are gathered with the performance event (that is, recorded immediately rather than two weeks after the activity).	
17. Measurement data are protected and audited to ensure the integrity of reported results.	
18. Scorecard data are reviewed regularly with those responsible for results.	
19. The method to communicate scorecard performance results to employees within the team and other stakeholders is effective.	
20. We regularly review the measures on our scorecard to ensure they are appropriate for our team's objectives, process responsibilities, and customers' expectations.	
Subtotal:	

Section C: Assessing Scorecard Content

Read each of the following statements. For each statement, rate your team's scorecard content using the following scale:

5 = Strongly Agree   2 = Disagree
4 = Agree   1 = Strongly Disagree
3 = Neither Agree nor Disagree

Section C: Scorecard Content	Rating (5 to 1)
21. Our team uses measures that monitor and evaluate success for our key business objectives.	
22. Our team's scorecard provides a balance of key indicators for financial achievements, process performance, customer satisfaction, and other key result areas.	
23. Historical trends, current levels, and desired targets are clear for each measure on our team's scorecard.	
24. Our scorecard provides a balance of input, process, and result measures.	
25. Our scorecard measures reflect changes from improvement actions taken by management or employees.	
26. Our scorecard measures provide a clear understanding of the performance capability of our systems and processes.	
27. We are able to quantify relationships between scorecard measures (for example, predict changes in revenues from customer satisfaction changes).	
28. Measures from front-line process teams are linked to management scorecards.	
29. Our team's scorecard measures are reliable; that is, they provide accurate and complete information.	
30. Our scorecard measures provide critical data for reviewing performance and supporting decision making.	
Subtotal:	

Score and Interpret Your Results

Total your scores from each section on the chart below.

Assessment Section	Score
A: Scorecard Alignment	
B: Scorecard Processes	
C: Scorecard Content	
Total:	

Scoring

- If your total score is between 125 and 150, your scorecard planning, content, and process are in good shape. You might need a few minor "tweaks" to your scorecard, but don't make major changes. Apparently, you have successfully developed and implemented effective measures.

- If your total score is between 75 and 124, examine your scorecard content and processes. Begin planning your next scorecard development cycle and be sure to involve the right people in refining your business objectives and scorecard measures.

- If your score is 74 or less, make a high priority of examining your scorecard measures. Contact other managers or external resources who can help you refine your measures and obtain the appropriate performance feedback for you and your team.

After fifteen minutes, Bob asked the managers to summarize their scores. Bob noted their reactions as they tallied their individual scores.

"Catherine and Miguel, you seemed to like what you saw from the assessment. Any comments?"

Catherine nodded, "I scored a 95, which is not great, but it's better than I thought, given that we're still learning. Looks like we're doing well with alignment, but need a little work on content and a lot on processes. We need to streamline our systems for gathering and reporting the help desk measures. They are too labor-intensive right now."

"Thanks, Catherine. How about you, Miguel?" Bob asked.

"We scored pretty well with an 88, but I realize from this that we haven't reviewed our measures with our suppliers. Most of our suppliers are internal, giving us work orders and specifications, so it should be fairly easy to do. Like Catherine, we didn't have a perfect score, but it looks as though we're moving in the right direction."

"Sounds great, Miguel, keep working on your refinements and talk with your suppliers. Anne, how did your scores turn out?"

"I won't even tell you our total score," Anne said with a grimace. "Now I'm worried that we got off to a bad start. We didn't do well in any area."

"Can you see any reason why?" Bob asked.

Anne glanced around at the rest of the team. "To be honest, I think it's because we tried to shortcut the process. We used measures for systems performance like network availability, mean time to repair, and other technical measures. But we really didn't factor in our customers' requirements or expectations. Also, we haven't been thorough in finding out our data for other indicators, like costs, customer satisfaction, and employee development. So it looks as if our next steps are to fill in these holes."

"All right, that's why you do an assessment," Bob said, "to identify areas to improve. Also, it's nice to know that this team has built enough trust that you can admit the need to improve. Max, how did yours turn out?"

"I thought we were doing everything right, but this survey slapped me in the face," Max said. "We have a lot of homework to do—everything from gathering measures more promptly, safeguarding the data, refining our supplier measures, and involving more people in our reviews. It's painful to admit, but I'm glad we did this survey. It looks like we don't have this scorecard stuff licked yet."

"That's why this phase is included in scorecard development," Bob explained. "Sometimes, initial results will lead you to believe that you're done. But a scorecard has to carry you for the long haul of your business, so you need a checkpoint with routine follow-ups to refresh your scorecard continually."

Bob continued, "You've already begun Step 2, to prioritize and act on your improvements. The most important thing here is to act on what you've discovered from your assessment. No scorecard is ever perfect; you just keep working on it to make it better.

> **Confirm**
> **Step 2**
> Prioritize and Act On Improvements

"As you've seen, your survey scores help you determine where you need refinements," Bob continued. "Reviewing responses to individual statements on the assessment enables you to pinpoint needed improvements. To turn the improvement opportunities into actions, define WHAT action is needed, WHO has responsibility for that action, and WHEN the action will start or stop. Your handout includes a worksheet that will help you define the improvement actions."

Bob's worksheet is shown below as Figure 8.2.

"Bob, since the survey is bringing out the truth about our scorecards, I have a confession to make," Vince said reluctantly. The managers turned to face Vince, who seemed embarrassed. "Although I like scorecards a lot, I have to admit that I haven't been able to get rid of all those old reports I used to go through. I don't

Action (What Needs to Happen)	Assignee (Who Will Do It)	Dates (When It Is Due)

Figure 8.2. *Actions Needed to Improve Scorecard Alignment, Processes, and Content*

use them anymore, but I can't seem to get rid of them. They are like a security blanket, and I'm worried that Jan Larson will ask me about them. Is that weird?"

Confirm

Step 3

Identify and Resolve
Measurement Issues

Bob smiled: "It's not weird. In fact, I've seen that behavior in almost every scorecard project. This is normal, as people react to change and performance monitoring. Measurement drives behavior, so your scorecard measures are signaling expected behavior changes. This is unsettling to some people, and you should expect concerns and issues. In fact, there are several issues you might anticipate when measurements improve. Step 3 of the Confirm Phase asks you to identify and resolve measurement issues."

"What are some of the other issues we might see?" Miguel asked.

"Glad you asked, because there is a summary in your handout," Bob said as the team laughed. "Some of these are attempts to slow or limit measurement. You will encounter people who resist measurement due to fear of the unknown or fear of exposure."

"Yeah, I have seen some of that from my team," Catherine agreed. "I wasn't sure how to handle it."

"We'll go through strategies for dealing with these issues in a moment," Bob said. "The good news is that many employees will provide ideas to improve your scorecards. You need to sort through attempts to limit measures and attempts to improve measures, all with the intent to stay focused on the reason for your measures—to improve business performance."

"Find the issues list in your handout, and let's go through them. As we go, put a check next to the behaviors or issues that you've seen so far," Bob said. The issues list Bob used is shown in Figure 8.3.

"There are many more issues that could arise, but these are the most prevalent ones. How did we do here? Which issues have you seen from your teams?" Bob said.

"This is very helpful, because I thought I was the only one going crazy," Anne said. "My work group that does specialized network designs insists it can't be measured. So far, I've left them alone. Sounds like they have the Prima Donna Syndrome. You think their work can be measured, Bob?"

"If they produce a work output of any sort, they can be measured," Bob said. "Start with a list of their outputs, customers' requirements, and work processes. Measures need to support the team's ability to deliver outputs, satisfy requirements, and manage its processes. Anyone else?"

"My integration testing work group seems to be in denial," Miguel said. "We've shown them results that indicate most tests are late and incomplete, but they say our data are wrong. I've checked and know it's not the data."

Issue	Description
Fear	Concern over how measures are used to evaluate team or individual performance, resulting in resistance to measurement.
Fudging	Manipulating results to achieve targets without actual changes to business results.
Finger Pointing	Blaming others and unrelated causes for performance problems.
Overreacting	Acting on normal variations in results, creating an unproductive spiral of actions, investigations, and process changes.
Prima Donna Syndrome	Insistence that the particular team activity is unique and cannot be measured.
Linus Syndrome	Named for the "Peanuts" cartoon character, this is refusal to eliminate the "security blanket" of obsolete measures.
Panacea Syndrome	Maintaining the belief that measures alone will fix performance problems, without the need to plan, review, check, and act.
Big Stick Syndrome	Using measures to "beat up" poorly performing managers instead of focusing on processes and managing improvements.
Denial	Refusal to accept the truth revealed by effective measures.
Hyperactivity	Measuring activities unrelated to actual and desired results.
Fuzz Factor	Complicating measures so that no one understands what is being measured.
Measure Mania	Cluttering scorecards with more measures than needed.

Figure 8.3. *Issues That May Surface During Scorecard Development*

"My second-shift help desk crew is so excited about our scorecard that they want to measure everything they do on their shift. I spotted them the other night measuring the number of times operators take breaks and how long the breaks are. They were doing it with a sense of fun to keep productivity up, but I thought it was a little excessive," Catherine said.

"Sounds like a bad case of Measure Mania," Max said. "I've seen some of that, too, but I seem to be having a problem with overreacting. My guys want to see the results three times per day and get really concerned when there are any downward blips. I can't seem to get them to realize that a little variation is expected and they shouldn't be overly alarmed. We're more interested in long-term improvements."

"Good, you're seeing that your teams are normal," Bob said. "Thanks for sharing those examples. Let me give you some strategies for how to deal with these behaviors. These are covered on the next page of your handout."

Bob continued, referring to the material shown in Figure 8.4, "From your observations, determine appropriate actions to address your scorecard issues. Most issues surface because people don't understand what is measured or why you are measuring. Communication is essential for resolving most issues. Depending on the severity of the situation and the impact on your team, here are some strategies to consider."

"These sound good, Bob," Vince said. "This helps us know that we're not crazy and need to continue to help our teams understand and use scorecards."

"Exactly," Bob concurred, "as you improve your scorecard, issues will continue to surface. This is normal. Over time, the issues will begin to focus on the need to update measures as changes occur to your business, your products, your customers, and your processes. Your final step in the Confirm

Confirm

Step 4

Establish a Process to Refine Your Scorecard Continually

Scorecard and Measurement Improvement Strategies

1. Make it clear that you are going to manage by fact and will use measures.
2. Ask for suggestions for refining measures.
3. Explain your scorecard to all members of your work team individually.
4. Invite all your team members to your next scorecard review.
5. Rotate team members through scorecard reviews on a regular cycle.
6. Go into work teams to explain the scorecard.
7. Explain the steps involved in reviews and what happens with results.
8. Display your scorecard publicly.
9. Have a scorecard publicity day during which various work team members explain parts of the scorecard.
10. Distribute your scorecard via "hard copy" or electronically.
11. Encourage feedback and discussion on the measures and current performance levels during breaks and lunch hours.
12. Post your scorecard on your company intranet.
13. Charter an "Action Team" to refine your measures.
14. Designate a team leader, besides yourself, who explains scorecard results to your team.
15. Give the team a deadline for improvement recommendations.
16. Designate someone from your team to verify scorecard results regularly. Rotate the assignment.
17. Train your team members on the proper interpretation and use of measures.
18. Involve your team members in setting targets.
19. Ask for improvements to measurement definitions, graphics, or targets.
20. Tie an incentive to the best measures (not necessarily the best results).

Figure 8.4. *Strategies for Addressing Scorecard Issues*

Phase is to establish an ongoing process for routinely handling scorecard changes."

"I'm sure you're going to explain all that," Anne remarked with a smile.

"Of course," Bob responded with a grin. "The scorecard change process requires three primary elements:

⇨ A *measurement lead* who serves as a focal point for measurement issues, questions, and proposed changes;

⇨ A *measurement steering team* to address measurement changes and issues; and

⇨ A *senior manager's* involvement and overview.

"The 'measurement lead' can be a manager, staff specialist, or supervisor who is assigned as the focal point for measurement issues," Bob explained. "The measurement lead resolves issues through management action or hands the issues to the measurement steering team. The measurement lead requires decision-making authority for issues that do not require involvement by the measurement steering team.

"The measurement steering team is composed of managers or representatives from the functions within your team. The team convenes when needed, usually no more than once per month. The steering team approves the system for gathering and reporting measures and reviews proposed changes for measures that affect the entire team. The steering team ensures the integrity of measurements and promotes the use of correct measures.

"The team's senior manager charters the measurement steering team and oversees the team's smooth operation. The senior manager may serve on the steering team. Recommendations or issues that cannot be handled by the steering team are given to the senior manager for resolution," Bob explained.

"I take it that I'm the senior manager you're referring to?" Vince asked.

"I believe you're it," Bob replied. "Your leadership is critical to making this successful. At the same time, you want your employees involved in raising and working the issues to refine measures continually and link the measures to improve business performance."

"Who would be on the steering team? All of us?" Miguel asked.

"I would suggest all of you, plus a few key lead employees. You want to promote ownership and involvement with them, too," Bob said.

Bob continued, "In your handout is a flow chart that shows a sample process for tying the three primary elements for managing measurement changes." Bob's flow chart is illustrated in Figure 8.5.

"Thanks for all your help, Bob," Vince said. "You've been an excellent guide for showing us how to make our scorecards a success. We'll follow through on our actions for addressing the issues and for setting up a change process. For now, I want to continue our celebration for what we've accomplished so far. I want to do that by treating our team and you to lunch. Agreed?"

"Meeting adjourned!" Bob exclaimed.

Summary

Issues, questions, and ideas will surface as you improve measures. During the Confirm Phase, you evaluate and refine your scorecard, establish a process for managing the issues, and involve the right people to refresh your scorecard continually. Focus actions toward improving measures to support better business performance and improving your team's ability to manage with measures. Keep your scorecard in line with business changes to ensure that your measurement data is relevant, fresh, and accurate.

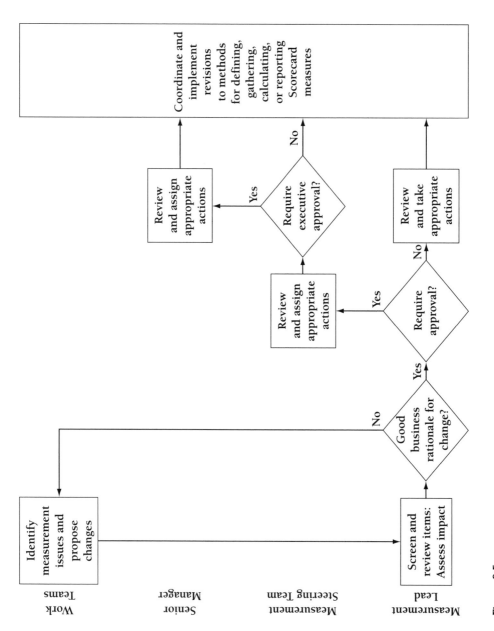

Figure 8.5. *A Process for Managing Measurement Changes*

PHASE	STEPS	OUTCOMES

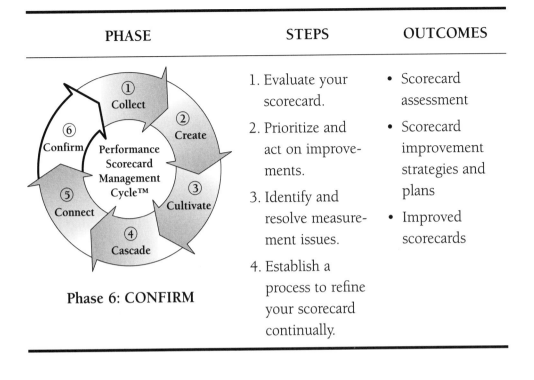

Phase 6: CONFIRM

1. Evaluate your scorecard.

2. Prioritize and act on improvements.

3. Identify and resolve measurement issues.

4. Establish a process to refine your scorecard continually.

- Scorecard assessment

- Scorecard improvement strategies and plans

- Improved scorecards

Measurement Case Study: Sears, Roebuck and Co.

An APQC Measurement Case Study

The rapid return to growth of Sears, Roebuck and Co. is a true corporate success story. Not surprisingly, Sears' measurement system contributed significantly to the turnaround. Measurement at Sears has matured to the point at which there is a clear link between employees' performance and profitability. Often the case with corporate makeovers, the turnaround began at a low point in Sears' long and distinguished history.

In 1992, Sears suffered a net loss of $3.9 billion. Its preeminence among retailers was replaced by Wal-Mart and K-Mart. Sears was in danger of going the way of other corporate giants that failed to change with the times. New leadership halted the disastrous "free fall" and guided Sears through a period of stabilization and restructuring that put the organization back on its feet. But the transformation was only beginning.

In 1994 top managers created a simple, but powerful vision for Sears to become:

⇨   A compelling place to work;

⇨   A compelling place to shop; and

⇨   A compelling place to invest.

This vision became the foundation for Sears' scorecard, known as the Total Performance Indicators (TPI), providing a powerful predictive tool that continuously tracks how well Sears delivers on each of the 3C's.

Through refinement, the TPI scorecard contributed immensely to Sears' financial turnaround and corporate transformation. At its center is a pervasive belief that shifts in associate and customer satisfaction measures translate into shifts in financial results that influence investor decisions. In other words, employee behavior affects customer satisfaction, which affects profits.

Through innovative means, Sears collects valuable data on each of the 3C's. Total Performance Indicators link "compelling place to work" with associate satisfaction. Annual surveys measure associate attitudes about their jobs and the company. Survey items explore topics such as work load, physical working conditions, treatment by supervisors, job fulfillment, company objectives, business strategy, and the company's future.

To determine whether Sears is a "compelling place to shop," a customer satisfaction survey is administered via an interactive voice response (IVR) system. Customers chosen at random receive a sales receipt with a printed coupon. They're encouraged to call a toll-free number to provide answers to twenty–plus questions about their Sears shopping experience. As an incentive, participating customers receive $5 off their next Sears purchase.

The IVR survey questions collect information about associate knowledge and availability, the shopping experience in general, and econometric/demographic data that's added to Sears' 90-plus–million-household database and used for marketing purposes.

"Compelling place to invest" measures track financial performance, including revenue growth, operating margin, and return on assets.

An employee-customer-profit model uses exacting calculations to predict performance outcomes with a great deal of accuracy. Sears uses sixteen quantifiable categories, such as advancement opportunities, training, salary, and benefits, to measure the associate side of the model. Each category is assigned a different point value because each has a larger or smaller influence on how associates feel about Sears as a "compelling place to work."

In its original statistical modeling, Sears determined that a five-point movement in the associate satisfaction category will affect overall associate satisfaction in a specific way. To illustrate, "advancement opportunities" has an assigned value of 1.3. If the advancement opportunities score goes up by five points, overall associate attitude about the job and company would also go up 1.3 points.

The payoff, financially speaking, comes when there is a five-point improvement in associate satisfaction. This translates into a 0.9 point improvement on average in customer satisfaction. Combine that with a 1 percent increase in customer retention, and Sears realizes a 1.3 percent improvement in revenue growth.

Sears continues to refine the system by fine-tuning the model to account for different associate and customer satisfaction dynamics within different parts of the store (e.g., apparel vs. major appliances). The company is developing a best-practice intranet library to share factors that lead to associate and customer satisfaction. Sears is also exploring other dimensions of the TPI measures, discovering that customers who rate their Sears shopping experience a perfect "10" will recommend Sears to a friend 96 percent of the time. When customers rate Sears a "9," they recommend Sears only 33 percent of the time.

The point is simple: There is a quantifiable relationship among the elements of a scorecard. Experience and analysis will help you discover the relationships between scorecard measures, leading to more effective decisions and business results.

"Associate, Customer Satisfaction Measures Fuel Sears' Model for Success," by Craig Henderson; *Measurement in Practice* (Third Quarter 1998) *Issue 13,* Houston, TX: American Productivity & Quality Center (APQC) © 1998. Reprinted with permission. Contact APQC for full text.

"The Employee-Customer-Profit Chain at Sears" by Anthony J. Rucci, Steven P. Kirn, and Richard T. Quinn, *Harvard Business Review* (January-February, 1998).

CHAPTER 9

Knowing the Score

....

In this chapter, Vince, Libby, and the rest of the team reflect on their progress and results. They realize the personal, professional, and organizational gains they've made and begin planning for scorecard and performance improvements in next year's business cycle. They review lessons learned and strategies for others to consider as they develop scorecards. Vince becomes a mentor for a vice president in another department just starting a scorecard, providing practical advice for handling measurement issues and helping his associate establish a process for developing and managing his scorecard.

Vince was treating his team to lunch at an elegant restaurant to celebrate the scorecard anniversary and the turnaround in business results. He felt the team worked hard to align its measures and promote the use and understanding of measures for improving business performance. Vince was feeling good, as Jan Larson noted the turnaround during her last staff meeting. In fact, a couple of the other vice presidents seemed to turn a jealous eye toward Vince's good fortune.

Vince felt it was far more than good fortune. He knew that his managers, despite some initial misgivings, had given their efforts wholeheartedly toward their success. Also, Vince felt that relationships and communication among his team had improved as a result of their alignment toward business objectives. Everyone seemed to be working together as a team, yet appreciating the unique contribution each member made. He was proud of them and what they had accomplished together.

After they ordered lunch, Vince called for a toast: "Here's to all of you for the results that we've achieved. I want to thank you all for the special effort you've given. I know it wasn't always easy. In fact, I'd like us to go around and share the most significant lesson learned during our scorecard efforts. Anne, would you like to start?"

"Sure," Anne replied. She thought for a moment and said, "I think the most valuable thing I learned was that measures can be used to challenge our teams. It's hard to set targets that challenge teams without setting targets so high that teams give up. But by working with customers and benchmarking, we can set targets that are achievable but require effort."

"Thanks, Anne," Vince said. "Miguel, how about you?"

"Sure, I've got an easy one," Miguel said. "Watch for number inflation. As you use measures, you may discover an inflated picture of performance. Give credit where due, but challenge values when things appear to be getting better with no apparent reason. I saw this a couple of times with one of my work groups. Once they saw I wasn't going to punish them for telling the truth, they began reporting numbers honestly. And results actually did get better."

"That is a good one, Miguel. I'd like to go next," Catherine said. "I realized that measures are more interrelated than I first thought. That is, an improvement in one measure is reflected by an improvement in another measure. For example, we saw errors go down in help desk calls, with reductions in costs and improvements in customer satisfaction. We expected it would happen, but it was exciting when it actually occurred. We learned to anticipate and look for relationships between measures. It's helped us make better decisions by knowing what to expect."

"That's great, Catherine. Max, any lessons learned?" Vince asked.

"There are so many, it's tough to pick just one," Max said. "I'd say the big one for me was: Don't take unnecessary actions. At first, my teams and I were tinkering with our processes too much, reacting to every little twitch in the measures. We were continually making adjustments until we realized our tinkering was actually making things worse. We were creating confusion and messing up procedures, actually adding costs and lowering performance. We had to stop and think about what we needed to do, isolate the action, and then monitor for the result. We actually learned to speed up by slowing down a little. Sounds crazy, but it worked for us."

"Wow, this had more effect than I thought it would. Holly, you've been quiet so far. What do you think is the greatest lesson?" Vince asked.

"I think it was the lesson Bob shared at this morning's meeting, that our scorecard is never done," Holly said. "We need to evolve measures as our business evolves. As we learn more about our customers' needs and our processes, we'll gain better understanding of the right measures. So, we'll always develop and refine measures as we go."

"Thanks, Holly," Vince said. "Now, my turn for a lesson learned. My greatest lesson is that I couldn't have done this without Libby. She got my attention when things looked really bad and suggested we use scorecards. I wasn't sure at first, but she's made a believer out of me. My hat is off to her with my special thanks."

The entire team applauded as Libby blushed and smiled. Just then, the server brought the lunches to the table. "Good, this saves me from giving a speech," Libby said to laughter. "Bob, how'd we do with our lessons learned?"

"On a scale of 1 to 10, I'd give you all a 12!" Bob said. The team applauded again and enjoyed the rest of their lunch together.

When Vince returned to the office, he had a message from Tim Parker, the vice president from SolvNET's Consulting Services Department. Vince and Tim were old friends from Vince's days with sales and marketing. Vince and Tim talked after Jan's staff meeting about the reaction from some vice presidents to Vince's turnaround. Vince wondered whether the new message was related as he dialed Tim's number.

Vince said, "Hello, Tim, this is Vince, returning your call."

"Hi, Vince, thanks for getting back," Tim replied. "I couldn't help but notice Jan's comments at our staff meeting about your big turnaround. I hear you've been fooling around with this scorecard stuff and wondered if they were connected."

Vince said, "The turnaround is definitely related to our use of scorecards. It's not just better measures, though. We made sure that our measures are tied to our business objectives and that we have our employees connected to our objectives using performance management. Why do you ask?"

"I just thought you might want to know that some people are saying that you're using scorecards just to highlight the results that you want to show," Tim said. "And others are wondering if your results are as good as they appear. You have to admit, the changes are pretty dramatic."

Vince replied angrily, "Now, wait, Tim, what are you implying?"

"I'm not implying anything, Vince, I'm just passing on information that I thought would help," Tim said. "I'm trying to do you a favor."

"Tim, I can assure you that our numbers are sound and that they represent the truth," Vince said. "My managers and I run checks to ensure the data is correct and we stand by the results."

"But, Vince, how can you be sure? You only show a few numbers. What happened to all the other results you used to track? Are they all doing as well?" Tim asked.

Vince replied, "We don't care about some of the results we used to track. We realized that some of our old measures never told us anything, so we dropped them. Other measures are now tracked in the work groups, where they belong. All of my managers are showing results with the measures linked to our business objectives. Those are the measures that matter, and those are the ones we monitor and report."

"You mean you actually got rid of some measures?" Tim asked. "How can that be possible?"

"Believe me, it was the best thing we did," Vince assured him. "It freed us to focus on the ones that really count and saved us time and resources to stop worrying about things that didn't matter or we couldn't control. Now, we feel like we're better managers and able to make better decisions."

"Vince, you're telling me that you're making better decisions with fewer measures?" Tim asked. "I feel like I never have enough information for my decisions. Tons of data, but no information."

Vince answered, "That's the whole point. Get rid of all the data that doesn't tell you anything and streamline down to your vital few measures. Align those measures to your business goals and keep them current. Review them regularly and make sure they are connected with your work groups. Make sure your work groups have the measures and feedback they need."

Tim said, "You make it sound so simple."

Vince said, "It is. It takes some effort to get coordinated, but it's worth it. It made us look closely at our business goals and how we align to SolvNET goals. By the time we were done, we knew how each employee on our customer services team contributed to our results. They knew it, too."

After a pause Tim asked, "How'd you do all that? That seems like a lot to figure out."

Vince said, "It's a simple six-step process. I'd be happy to show you how."

"Sure, I'd really like to know," Tim said. "If your results are legitimate and, knowing you, they are, I'd sure like to get in on the secret."

Vince continued, "It's no secret at all. Want to have lunch tomorrow and talk about it?"

"You bet. My treat," Tim answered.

Vince laughed, "Now, you're talking. I'll pick you up at noon."

As they concluded their call, Vince felt especially good for his team. Tim was a good manager, and it was significant that he had asked for help. Maybe others in SolvNET wanted to know about Performance Scorecards. He turned his chair toward the window and began daydreaming about what it might be like for Jan Larson and all the others to use scorecards. He recalled his discussion with her during the Create Phase and felt there was a glimmer of interest. He could just see SolvNET corporate results go through the ceiling.

"Vince, are you ready for your two o'clock meeting?" Vince's reverie was broken by Libby at the door.

"Sure, Libby. Refresh me. What's the topic?"

"Next year's business plans. Jan Larson wants to share with you next year's business goals. I hear through the grapevine that she's going to have some surprises and some pretty tough targets."

Vince looked at Libby squarely: "Libby, it's our turn to surprise her. The SolvNET customer services team is ready for tough targets—and any other challenge she wants to give us. In fact, I'll surprise her after the meeting with a one-on-one discussion on scorecards. We could make things a lot better around here."

Libby laughed: "We'll need to track a measure of your success with Jan. Good luck!"

Summary

Developing scorecards requires effort, but delivers a return on investment by providing fewer, better measures that provide the right information for the real world. Management teams are strengthened as scorecards help teams unite efforts toward common business goals, providing feedback that encourages and reinforces desired performance.

The following occurs when management teams use scorecards to regularly review results:

⇨ Performance changes (positive and negative) are quickly noted;

⇨ Trends are easily recognized;

⇨ Root causes for performance swings are identified;

⇨ Appropriate actions are determined;

⇨ Problems are prevented from growing;

⇨ Performance improvements are reinforced; and

⇨ Management "fire-fighting" is reduced.

Follow the steps to developing, managing, and using scorecards to drive business performance. You'll be following the steps that other companies and individuals have used to reduce frustration and achieve better results.

References

Baldrige National Quality Program. (January 1999). *Board of Examiners Update.* Gaithersburg, MD: National Institute of Standards and Technology.

Baldrige National Quality Program. (1999). *Malcolm Baldrige National Quality Award: Profiles of Winners.* Gaithersburg, MD: National Institute of Standards and Technology.

Canik, A. (1997, October/November). *Aggressive performance management and measurement pay off: City of Indianapolis pioneers privatization.* Houston, TX: American Productivity & Quality Center.

Daniels, S., & Hagen, M. (1999, April). Making the pitch in the executive suite: How quality got to the top with six Baldrige Award winners. *Quality Progress,* pp. 25–33.

Elliott, S. (1997, August/September). *Measuring success: Winning the Baldrige was just a step along Granite Rock's endless road to quality.* Houston, TX: American Productivity & Quality Center.

Henderson, C. (1998). *Associate, customer satisfaction measures fuel Sears' model for success.* Houston, TX: American Productivity & Quality Center.

Henderson, C. (1998). *Innovative measurement systems: A way of life at Bekaert UBISA.* Houston, TX: American Productivity & Quality Center.

Heskett, J., Jones, T., Loveman, G., Sasser, W., & Schlesinger, L. (1994, March/April). Putting the service-profit chain to work. *Harvard Business Review,* pp. 164–174.

Kaplan, R., & Norton, D. (1993, September/October). Putting the balanced scorecard to work. *Harvard Business Review,* pp. 73–87.

Kaplan, R., & Norton, D. (1996). *The Balanced Scorecard.* Boston, MA: Harvard Business School Press.

Landes, L. (1995, July). Leading the Duck at Mission Control. *Quality Progress,* pp. 43–45.

Lingle, J., & Schiemann, W. (1996, March). From balanced scorecard to strategic gauges: Is measurement worth it? *Management Review,* pp. 56–61.

Morgan, B., & Schiemann, W. (1999, January). Measuring people and performance: Closing the gaps. *Quality Progress,* pp. 47–53.

Rucci, A., Kirn, S., & Quinn, R. (1998, January/February). The employee-customer-profit chain at Sears. *Harvard Business Review,* pp. 83–97.

Strategic plans don't produce desired results. (1996, June). *Quality Progress,* p. 22.

Stratton, B. (1998, October). Texas Nameplate Company: All you need is trust. *Quality Progress,* pp. 29–32.

Stratton, B. (1998, October). UPS: Its long-term design delivers quality millions of times each day. *Quality Progress,* pp. 37–38.

Struebing, L. (1996, December). Measuring for excellence. *Quality Progress,* pp. 25–28.